SPIRITUAL WARFARE

A CENTRE FOR PENTECOSTAL THEOLOGY SHORT INTRODUCTION

SPIRITUAL WARFARE

A CENTRE FOR PENTECOSTAL THEOLOGY SHORT INTRODUCTION

Opoku Onyinah

CPT Press
Cleveland, Tennessee

SPIRITUAL WARFARE
A Centre for Pentecostal Theology Short Introduction

Published by CPT Press
900 Walker ST NE
Cleveland, TN 37311
USA
email: cptpress@pentecostaltheology.org
website: www.cptpress.com

Library of Congress Control Number: 2011937201

ISBN-10: 1935931210
ISBN-13: 9781935931218

Dedicated to the memory of Mrs Gladys Yamoah
(who died on 8 April 2007)

TABLE OF CONTENTS

PART FOUR
THE WEAPONS OF OUR WARFARE

SERIES PREFACE

The Centre for Pentecostal Theology Short Introductions are monographs that offer a distinctively Pentecostal perspective on various topics that are of relevance to the movement. Based on current and sound research, these short books are designed to introduce the reader to the topic at hand while not overwhelming him or her with all the secondary literature on the subject. The goal is a straightforward introduction with helpful assessments by leading scholars in the tradition.

ACKNOWLEDGEMENTS

I was researching spiritual warfare when Rev Jeff Korum asked me to present a paper on the subject at 'Awaken to the World', a programme in Accra, Ghana that equips pastors and church leaders in missions. Afterward, the numerous requests for the audio cassette of the presentation and the desire of the participants to have more insight into the subject hastened the writing of this book. I am thankful to Jeff for giving me the initial assignment and for editing this book.

I am also grateful to Rev Jeff Koram, Elders Gibson Annor-Antwi, J.M.K. Nyaadie, Mrs Trish Waller, and Mrs Ohui Agbenyega Allotey for editing and proofreading. Again I am thankful to Ms Dorcas Wuni, Faustina Enninful, and Mr Kwasi Annor for providing secretarial assistance.

Over the years in ministry, as I endured my share of spiritual warfare, I received immense support from diverse people, including my parents, siblings, and friends. I am grateful to all of them. Among them was Mrs Gladys Yamoah (alias Yaa Kyerewah) and her family, Elder Eric, Isaac, Gideon, Debora, Tryphena, and Tryposa. Gladys died on 8 April 2007, and she was a beloved sister to me. Often in my research travels I would rest at her home with her family, and I found refreshment. I dedicate this book to her memory.

For their time, understanding, sacrifice, and support offered me over the years in my ministry, I register my sincerest appreciation to my wife Grace and our children – Mark, Daniel, Caleb, Grace, Nicholas, and Stephen.

INTRODUCTION

Theology should be meaningful to laypeople as well as to practising pastors. Academia should be in touch with the world it is trying to reach. The work of theologians should serve the needs of the Church. With that goal, I want this book to suit practising preachers as well as academia. This is a difficult task, because what the theologians want is often different from what preachers need in their churches. How can we make the efforts of academics more relevant to church situations? That question is important to me. As a theologian and also a pastor who has been recognised and called to the apostleship by my denomination, I want this book to be a fresh, biblical look at the subject of spiritual warfare, and I hope that it will meet the needs of both the scholarly and pastoral worlds. Of course, there is nothing new under the sun (Eccl. 1.9). What I do here is to highlight a viewpoint which has been neglected.

I have reviewed the existing practices and literature on the subject, and I address the concerns that the contemporary approaches raise. In addition, I draw a lot from my ongoing pastoral experience and offer pastoral treatment as well. Some examples are cited from research I conducted in 1999. Based upon all these, I offer suggestions that I think are healthy and biblical for the promotion of Christ and his Church.

Part One comprises Chapters One, Two, and Three. Here, I present the theology of demonology from early Pentecostalism to contemporary times. I explain what is meant by territorial warfare, including ground-level warfare and strategic-level warfare. I show the positive aspects of this contemporary approach as well as the problems that come along with it. This part of the book, therefore, may not be very interesting for lay practitioners of spiritual warfare. I shall therefore request such people to jump to Part Two. However, if such people desire to know more about the contemporary approaches and the problems they raise, they should read this section.

There are two chapters in Part Two: Chapters Four and Five. In Chapter Four, I define spiritual warfare by examining what the Bible says on the subject. After this, I look at the victories that Christ has won. Here I examine the temptation of Christ in the wilderness, the significance of Christ's death and resurrection, and their implications for the believer.

Part Three comprises Chapters Six to Thirteen. These form the study of the strongholds of the devil. In Chapter Six, false doctrines are presented as one of the devil's weapons against Christianity. Among other things, I describe how false teachings emerge. Chapter Seven is a study of the flesh, and why it, rather than the demonic, is contrasted with the Spirit in the Bible. In Chapter Eight, I look at the postmodern world, with its pluralism of beliefs and practices, including all the varieties of sexual freedom and the troublesome filth in the media. Chapter Nine analyses the New Age Movement and the New World Order. In Chapter Ten, I describe occult activities such as divination, spiritism, sorcery, witchcraft, astral projection, and witchdemonology. In Chapter Eleven, I present murder as one of the strongholds the devil capitalises on in the contemporary world. Chapter Twelve shows Satanism as another stronghold of the devil. The summary of the section is presented in Chapter Thirteen.

Part Four highlights the weapons of our warfare. This is from Chapter Fourteen to the end. The available weapons – the belt of truth, the breastplate of righteousness, shoes of the gospel, the shield of faith, the helmet of salvation, the sword of the spirit, the ministry of the word, the sharing of testimony, prayer, praise, and worship – are all explained in turn. In this section, I also discuss deliverance and whether or not Christians can be possessed. I wrote this section as if I were teaching in a church setting so that the material will be relevant to local congregations.

The conclusions bring together the salient discoveries of the book. Significantly, these repeat verbatim some issues that have been touched on already. The reason is to remind the reader of what has been pointed out already. May the Lord bless you and give you more insight as you study this book.

PART ONE

THE NATURE OF SPIRITUAL WARFARE

1

WHAT PEOPLE SAY ABOUT SPIRITUAL WARFARE

A charismatic renewal swept through world Christianity in the latter part of the twentieth century, beginning in the 1960s. In this renewal, distinct Pentecostal blessings and phenomena occurred outside classic Pentecostal churches. This phenomena included what is commonly called the baptism of the Holy Spirit with speaking in tongues, healings, and prophesying. Out of this came a new awareness of Satan, demons, and other powers of evil. Consequently, we saw an increase in deliverance ministries, breaking of demonic strongholds, and exorcisms.

This is not to say that the issue of demonology or confronting the powers of evil was absent in Pentecostalism. Dealing with the demonic arose with the Pentecostal revival in the beginning of the twentieth century, as has been rightly observed by Stephen Hunt, 'The growth and appeal of deliverance came with the expansion of the "classical" Pentecostal movement at the beginning of the twentieth century.'[1] However, the emphasis in this early period was on speaking in tongues as an initial evidence of the baptism of the Holy Spirit and as a powerful weapon for evangelism; healing and deliverance were to accompany the baptism.[2] The belief was that the

---

[1] Stephen Hunt, 'Managing the Demonic: Some Aspects of the Neo-Pentecostal Deliverance Ministry', *Journal of Contemporary Religion* 13.2 (1998), p. 216.

[2] For example, see Allan Anderson, 'Signs and Blunders: Pentecostal Mission Issues at Home and Abroad in the 20th Century', *Asian Journal of Missions* 2.2 (2000), pp. 193-210; Walter J. Hollenweger, *Pentecostalism: Origins and Developments*

name of Jesus was powerful enough to crush the kingdom of Satan. For example, the Norwegian historian of Pentecostalism, Bloch-Hoell, wrote that Satan and his kingdom occupied a place in the Pentecostal message on supernatural healing, but this was mainly 'in the appeal for the winning of souls and in holiness preaching'.[3]

Consequently many Pentecostal churches did not believe a Christian could be possessed by demons. One significant example is the USA Assemblies of God, which teaches that a born-again Christian could never be indwelt by an evil spirit.[4] Some Pentecostal churches therefore opposed those who attempted to make deliverance a specialty.[5]

Yet, as is usually the case, they could not cramp the activities of popular itinerant healing and deliverance ministries that sprang up on the perimeter of the movement. For such Pentecostals, as Keith Warrington observes, 'Their view of the demonic owes as much to medieval art and popular fiction as it does to the New Testament.'[6] For many of those practitioners, the experiences and testimonies during 'deliverance services', rather than the New Testament, became the source of beliefs concerning the devil and demons.

Though many Pentecostals adhered to the biblical doctrines of demonology, certain writers strayed outside that framework. Thus, Warrington observes that 'the lack of biblical parameters for much of that which is written makes the exercise subjective, and, at times,

---

Worldwide (Peabody: Hendrickson, 1997), pp. 18-24; Benny C. Aker, 'The Gospel in Action', in *Signs and Wonders in Ministry Today* (Benny C. Aker and Gary S. McGee, eds.; Springfield: Gospel Publishing House, 1996), pp. 35-45; Robert Mapes Anderson, *Vision of the Disinherited: The Making of American Pentecostalism* (Oxford: Oxford University Press, 1979), pp. 79-80; Charles W. Conn, *Like a Mighty Army: A History of the Church of God* (Cleveland: Pathway Press, 1977), p. 92; Frederick Dale Bruner, *A Theology of the Holy Spirit: The Pentecostal Experience and the New Testament Witness*, 2nd ed. (London: Hodder & Stoughton, 1972), pp. 47-55.

[3] Nils Bloch-Hoell, *The Pentecostal Movement: Its Origin, Development, and Distinctive Character* (London: Allen & Unwin, 1964), p. 111.

[4] Hunt, 'Managing the Demonic', p. 217; Steven S. Carter, 'Demon Possession and the Christian', *Asian Journal of Pentecostal Studies* 3.1 (2000), p. 19; William K. Kay, *Inside Story: A History of British Assemblies of God* (Mattersey: Mattersey Hall Publishing, 1999), p. 337.

[5] Hunt, 'Managing the Demonic', p. 217; Carter, 'Demon Possession and the Christian', p. 19.

[6] Keith Warrington, 'Healing and Exorcism: The Path to Wholeness', in *Pentecostal Perspective* (Keith Warrington, ed.; Carlisle: Paternoster Press, 1998), pp. 171-72.

suspect, leaving a trail of speculation and confusion for the readers.[7] From such unsettled beliefs in Pentecostal circles, Walter Hollenweger, the doyen of theological studies, concludes that the matter of demonology is 'an unsolved problem in Pentecostal belief and practice'.[8] Because of this confusion, teachers of spiritual warfare in the charismatic renewal had lots of room to operate.

These charismatic teachers arose in the 1970s through the early 1990s, and they tried to explain the powers of Satan and how to exorcise them. Some prominent evangelists, pastors, and authors who practiced deliverance were Derek Prince, Don Basham, Fred Dickason, Charles Kraft, Kurt Koch, Mark Bubeck, Bill Subritsky, John Wimber, and Francis MacNutt.[9] What can be deduced from these writers is that one could be a Christian, baptised in the Holy Spirit, speak in tongues – yet still have demons or be plagued by various curses until the Holy Spirit revealed them and dealt with them. Casting out a demon or renouncing a curse could be a lengthy process, and it was only forceful men who could practice it.

Books written by former witches and people who had been demon possessed were also popular at this time. Doreen Irvine's book, *From Witchcraft to Christ*, was a popular one. Irvine wrote that after becoming involved in Satanism and witchcraft, she underwent a long exorcism before receiving her deliverance. While in Satanism,

---

[7] Warrington, 'Healing and Exorcism', p. 172.
[8] Walter J. Hollenweger, *The Pentecostals* (London: SCM Press Ltd, 1972), p. 379.
[9] Derek Prince, *Blessings or Cursing* (Milton Keynes: Word Publishing, 1990); *From Cursing to Blessing* (Lauderdale: Derek Prince Ministries, 1986); *They Shall Expel Demons: What You Need to Know about Demons: Your Invisible Enemies* (Harpenden: Derek Prince Ministries, 1998); Don Basham, *Can a Christian Have a Demon?* (Monroeville: Whitaker House, 1971); C. Fred Dickason, *Demon Possession and the Christian* (Chicago: Moody Press, 1987); Charles. H. Kraft, *Defeating Dark Angels* (Kent: Sovereign World, 1993); John Wimber with Kevin Springer, *Power Evangelism* (London: Hodder and Stoughton, 1992); Kurt E. Koch, *Occult Bondage and Deliverance* (Grand Rapids: Kregel Publications, 1970); Kurt E. Koch, *Demonology, Past and Present*, (Grand Rapids: Kregel Publications, 1981). Mark I. Bubeck, *Overcoming the Adversary* (Chicago: Moody Press, 1984); Mark I. Bubeck, *The Adversary* (Chicago: Moody Press, 1975); Bill Subritsky, *Demons Defeated* (Chichester: Sovereign World, 1986); John Wimber and Kevin Springer, *Power Healing* (London: Hodder & Stoughton, 1988); Francis MacNutt, *Deliverance from Evil Spirits: A Practical Manual* (London: Hodder & Stoughton, 1995); Ed Murphy, *The Handbook for Spiritual Warfare*, rev. ed., (Nashville: Thomas Nelson Publishing, 1996).

the phrase 'blood of Jesus' tormented her.[10] Rebecca Brown's works, including *He Came to Set the Captives Free,* also became very popular.[11] This book presented the clash between Elaine, who was said to be one of the top witches in the USA, and Brown, a medical doctor who was a Christian. Elaine was said to be so powerful that she could destroy Christian churches. In the struggle to save Elaine's life, Brown nearly lost her own. In the end, Elaine finally left Satan to accept Christ.

In Africa, one of the books which became very popular was *Delivered from the Powers of Darkness* by the Nigerian preacher Emmanuel Eni. The fact that it was published by Scripture Union contributed to the book's widespread appeal.[12] In vivid, dramatised form, Eni wrote how he became involved in the occult. He claimed to be an agent of the Queen of the Coast (Maami Wata or water deity), who met Satan personally and was often sent to attack Christians. He presented the immense struggles that took place between the powers in him and a group of Assemblies of God church members who sought to deliver him. The blood of Jesus scared the demons. Eni revealed that most of the products and inventions that were sold in the markets were engineered and designed by demons. Buying and using them attracted demons to people.

These books all portray Satan as real and powerful – and he will eventually ensnare all of us in his wicked devices because the environment is so full of demonic activities and products. Further, the books teach that to overpower him (Satan), Christians must engage in a genuine battle with his kingdom.[13] The primary weapon in

---

[10] Doreen Irvine, *From Witchcraft to Christ: My True Life Story* (London: Concordia Press, 1973), p. 124.

[11] Rebecca Brown, *He Came to Set the Captives Free* (Springdale: Whitaker House, 1992). See also other books by Brown: *Prepare for War* (Springdale: Whitaker House, 1987); *Becoming a Vessel of Honour* (Springdale: Whitaker House, 1990); *Unbroken Curses: Hidden Source of Trouble in the Christian's Life* (Springdale: Whitaker House, 1995).

[12] Emmanuel Eni, *Delivered from the Powers of Darkness,* (Ibadan: Scripture Union, 1987). See also Birgit Meyer, 'Delivered from the Powers of Darkness: Confessions of Satanic Riches in Christian Ghana', *Africa* 65.2 (1995), pp. 237-55.

[13] Brown states that during the eight week period that she was trying to exorcise Elaine, neither she nor Elaine 'had more than one to two hours of unbroken sleep per night' (Brown, *He Came to Set the Captive Free,* p. 105). What makes the presentation of Brown so terrifying is that the 'battle', as she calls it, began a week after Elaine's first deliverance or deliverance session. There was a real 'battle' (several prayers of deliverance) before Elaine was set free (pp. 105-36).

overpowering him is repeatedly invoking the blood and name of Jesus. Although all these books were testimonies of new Christians who were sharing their subjective experiences, the manner in which they received their freedom became a model for others.

2

TERRITORIAL WARFARE

In the final decade of the twentieth century, the focus changed from demon possession to levels of spiritual warfare. Two scholars who led the way were Charles Kraft and Peter Wagner; they are often labeled as 'Third Wave' or 'Neo-Charismatic' theologians. They teach that there are two levels of warfare: Ground-level and cosmic-level. Kraft is more concerned about ground-level,[14] while Wagner is concerned about cosmic level, which he calls strategic-level warfare.[15]

Ground-Level Warfare

Ground-level warfare deals with evil spirits that inhabit people. These spirits are classified into three kinds. The first is family spirits or ancestral spirits, which gained their power through successive generations of children up to the current generation. They are considered the most powerful of all the ground-level demons. The second is the occult spirits. These are the demons of all non-Christian religions and cults, and they gain their power through invitation.

---

[14] Charles H. Kraft, *Defeating the Dark Angels* (Kent: Sovereign World, 1993); Charles H. Kraft, *Christianity with Power* (Ann Arbor, MI: Servant, 1989).

[15] C. Peter Wagner, *Warfare Prayer* (Ventura: Regal, 1991); C. Peter Wagner, *Warfare Prayer: How to Seek God's Power and Protection in the Battle to Build His Kingdom* (Ventura: Regal, 1992); C. Peter Wagner, ed., *Engaging the Enemy: How to Fight and Defeat Territorial Spirits* (Ventura: Regal, 1993); C. Peter Wagner, *Confronting the Powers: How the New Testament Church Experienced the Power of Strategic Level Spiritual Warfare* (Ventura: Regal, 1996); Peter Wagner was once a Professor of Mission at Fuller Theological Seminary.

The third class is the ordinary demons. These are attached to such vices as anger, fear, lust, death, gambling, drunkenness, pornography, fornication, and homosexuality.

Third-wave theologians say that people who are inhabited by one or more of these spirits are 'demonised', a word they prefer to demon possession. This term is based upon the Greek word *daimonizomai* which simply means 'have a demon'. The objective is to expose the demon and cast it out in Jesus' name.

Strategic-Level Warfare

Strategic-level warfare is considered to have at least five types. First are the territorial spirits who are said to be over cities, regions, and nations. This assumption is heavily based on Dan. 10.13, 21 where the Prince of Persia and the Prince of Greece are mentioned. Territorial spirits are defined as 'high-ranking members of the hierarchy of evil spirits who are dispatched by Satan to control nations, regions, cities, tribes, people groups, neighbourhoods, and other significant social networks'. Second are the institutional spirits, and they are assigned to non-Christian religions, governments, churches, and educational institutions. Third are the spirits responsible for supervising and promoting special functions and vices such as prostitution, abortion, homosexuality, music, pornography, media, and war. Fourth are those assigned to objects like buildings, tools, and instruments, as well as nonmaterial entities like rituals and practices. These demons receive their assignments at formal dedication ceremonies. Fifth are ancestral spirits that rule over specific families, and they can assume the identity of the ancestors themselves.

Strategic-level spirits are in charge of ground-level spirits and assign them to people and supervise their work. In order to break the powers of these spirits one must engage in genuine 'spiritual warfare', which Wagner calls strategic-level warfare.[16] At the heart of this warfare is Wagner's threefold strategy: 1) discerning the territo-

---

[16] Wagner, *Warfare Prayer*. Wagner presents the comprehensive detail of this strategy in this book. See also Gwen Shaw, *Redeeming the Land: A Bible Study on Dislodging Evil Spirits, Breaking the Curse and Restoring God's Blessing Upon the Land* (Japer, Arkansas: Engeltal Press, 1987). The publication of this book preceded Wagner's, yet they shared similar ideas.

rial spirits; 2) dealing with the corporate sin of a city; and 3) engaging in aggressive warfare against the territorial spirits.[17]

Advocates of Wagner's ministry have echoed this approach. Regarding the first step, George Otis, Jr. writes that 'spiritual mapping' is necessary for discerning the territorial spirits assigned to a city.[18] This technique is used to discern and identify the spirits over the territory as a step toward developing strategies to combat and defeat them.

John Dawson popularized the second part of the strategy, dealing with the corporate sin of a city or an area. Dawson coined the expression 'identification repentance' to explain the need of repenting and then confessing these sins as a means of effecting reconciliation, thus breaking Satan's grip.[19] Wagner remarked, 'No aspect of warfare prayer is more important than identification repentance'.[20]

The third part of strategic-level warfare – engaging in an aggressive struggle against the territorial spirits – was heightened by Cindy Jacobs.[21] Christians engage in 'casting down strongholds', 'binding the strongman', 'evicting the ruler of the city', 'storming the gates of hell', and 'taking dominion in Jesus' name'.

Positive Results of Spiritual Warfare

This threefold practice has gained growing popularity among Christians worldwide, and it has produced some positive results. For example, it has sparked many Christians to strategise, plan, and pray effectively before evangelism. The result is that the gospel has been

[17] C. Peter Wagner, *Confronting the Powers: How the New Testament Church Experienced the Power of Strategic Level Spiritual Warfare* (Ventura: Regal, 1996).

[18] George Otis Jr. is the president of Sentinel Group and coordinator with Wagner of AD 2000 & Beyond Movement's United Prayer Track. He heads the Spiritual Mapping Division. See George Otis Jr., *The Last of the Giants: Lifting the Veil on Islam and the End Times* (Grand Rapids: Chosen, 1993), p. 32; George Otis Jr., 'An Overview of Spiritual Mapping', in *Breaking Strongholds in Your City: How to Use Spiritual Mapping to Make Prayers More Strategic, Effective, and Targeted* (C. Peter Wagner, ed.; Ventura: Regal, 1991), p. 85.

[19] See John Dawson, *Taking Our Cities for God: How to Break Spiritual Strongholds* (Lake Mary: Creation House, 1989), pp. 183-89.

[20] Wagner, *Confronting the Powers*, pp. 249-50.

[21] Cindy Jacobs is the president of Generals of Intercession, based in Colorado Springs, Colorado. Cindy Jacobs, *Possessing the Gates of the Enemy: A Training Manual for Militant Intercession* (Grand Rapids: Chosen, 1994), pp. 245-46; Cindy Jacobs, 'Dealing with Stronghold', in *Breaking Strongholds in Your City*.

preached in difficult areas, and the church has grown. An example is Argentina, where a missions team experienced an evangelistic breakthrough after intense prayer. John Dawson said the success was the result of breaking the demonic stronghold over the city.[22]

In addition, there has been renewed focus on the area that is described as the '10/40 Window'. Luis Bush coined this term to describe the spiritually barren nations between the latitudes of 10 and 40 degrees north.[23] This area comprises a high percentage of the world's least-evangelised peoples. George Otis, Jr. says this is the last remaining stronghold of demonic possession, and he points out that the Garden of Eden (Iran and Iraq) are at the centre of 10/40 Window. When this area is reached, God will wind down the historical process and bring closure to world evangelisation. To bring this to pass, evangelistic forces currently surrounding the Window must continue their advance at a more or less uniform pace.[24] Because of all the attention on this area of the world, it has received a renewed mission focus.

Spiritual warfare has also stirred many to identify various problems and pray about them. Thus, intercession in Christian ministries has intensified. For example, many teach that the real sources of African problems are the controlling powers of various territorial spirits, such as the spirits of poverty and idolatry. What initially opened the door for demons was Africans' involvement in the slave trade with all of its bloodshed. Some African scholars such as Professor Oshun and 'Evangelist' Nwankpa have stressed the need to wage 'spiritual warfare' against these spiritual enemies to break free the African continent.[25] From these teachings, Maxwell rightly observes that, for the African, the answer to the continental problem of poverty is to be 'delivered from the spirit of poverty'.[26] Many

---

[22] Dawson, *Taking Our Cities for God,* p. 20; Tommy Lea, 'Spiritual Warfare and the Missionary Task', in *Missiology* (John Mark Terry, Ebbie Smith, Justice Anderson, eds.; Nashville: Broadman & Holman, 1998), pp. 628-29.

[23] Mike Wakely, 'Territorial Spirits: Some Concerns Expressed by Mike Wakely', Operation Mobilization (18.7.93).

[24] Mike Wakely, 'Territorial Spirits'.

[25] See Emeka Nwankpa, *Redeeming the Land: Interceding for the Nations* (Achimota: African Christian Press, 1994), p. 9; Chris O. Oshun, 'Spirits and Healing in a Depressed Economy: The Case of Nigeria', *Mission Studies* 25.1 (1998), p. 33.

[26] David Maxwell, 'Delivered from the Spirit of Poverty? Pentecostalism, Prosperity and Modernity', *Journal of Religion in Africa* 28.3 (1998), pp. 350-73.

churches and intercessory prayer ministries have responded by es-
tablishing powerful national and international prayer ministries to
intercede for Africans. Africa-wide intercessory bodies include Intercessors for Africa, AD 2000 Prayer Track, and Praying Through
The Window.[27]

Another positive development from spiritual warfare is that the
evil of sin has been exposed. Even within the charismatic renewal,
some Christians took many vices lightly. Because of the warfare focus, vices such as smoking, pornography, sexual self-gratification,
and gambling are considered sins that have demonic attachments.
Thus Christians are taught to avoid such things.

Finally, contemporary spiritual warfare teachings have challenged
Christians to reinvigorate their faith and practice it more vibrantly.
Spiritual warfare practitioners report miracles at their services, but
conventional churches rarely make that claim.

---

[27] See Ogbu U. Kalu, 'The Third Response: Pentecostalism and the Reconstruction of Christian Experience in Africa, 1970-1995', *Journal of African Christian
Thought* 1.2 (December 1998), p. 13.

3

THE PROBLEMS WITH CONTEMPORARY SPIRITUAL WARFARE TEACHINGS

They Give Too Much Attention to the Demonic World

A serious problem with modern spiritual warfare teachings is that they give too much attention to Satan. Some scholars, especially Sociologist Harvey Cox and New Testament scholar Robert Guelich, have rightly pointed out that the basis for much contemporary spiritual warfare, with its excessive interest in demonic hierarchy, is Frank Peretti's novel *This Present Darkness* rather than the word of God.[28]

The Bible clearly indicates that Satan rules over a hierarchy of evil spirits who attempt to control territories on earth. This is the picture given at Dan. 10.13, 20-21. The unnamed angel of God was resisted by the Prince of Persia until Michael came to assist him (Dan. 10.13). This angel informed Daniel, 'Do you know why I have come to you? And now I must return to fight with the prince of Persia; and when I have gone forth, indeed the prince of Greece will come' (Dan. 10.20).

This is an indication that there are princes from Satan attached to kingdoms or territories. But the Bible does not show that the people of God have the power to dispel these evil spirits from their

---

[28] Harvey Cox, *Fire From Heaven: The Rise of Pentecostal Spirituality and the Reshaping of Religion in the Twenty-First Century* (London: Cassell, 1996), pp. 281-84; Robert A. Guelich, 'Spiritual Warfare: Jesus, Paul and Peretti', *PNEUMA* 13.1 (1991), pp. 33-64; Frank Peretti, *This Present Darkness* (Westchester: Crossway Book, 1986), p. 34.

kingdoms. Christians have the authority to cast out evil spirits from people (Mk 16.17; Lk. 10.17-19; Acts 5.16; 8.7; 16.18). Also, Christians can resist the devil from taking control of their lives (Jas 4.7; 1 Pet. 5.8-9). However, there is no example of God's people pulling down the princes or evil spirits over cities. It is not possible.

In the Bible, demonic powers are reduced to secondary causes in the accomplishment of God's supreme purpose. There is no detailed description of Satan's activities, neither are there detailed confessions of demoniacs as we have in modern deliverance services.

Finally, the Bible does not provide any detailed rituals or techniques for identifying problems or performing exorcisms. Some modern expressions and techniques (such as spiritual mapping, ground-level warfare, cosmic-level warfare, and evicting the ruler of this city), and some practices during exorcisms (such as the emphasis on prayer language, the role of repetitive and intensive prayer, the need for fasting, and the demand for confession) seem to reduce spiritual warfare to mere magical techniques rather than confidence in God himself.

They Fail to Consider the Sovereignty of God

In the Bible, the Lord is the one true God, with supremacy over all spiritual powers (Deut. 6.4; 33.2-3; Neh. 9.6; Job 38-39; Ps. 89.5-8; Ps. 148.1-13; Eph. 4.4-6). Satan is simply one of the spirits (Job 1.6-7), and these spirits, whether good or evil, remain under God's sovereignty.

Satan and his spirits can only tempt or afflict by divine permission (Job 1.12; Mt. 4.1; Lk. 22.31; 2 Cor. 12.7). They can be used by God to accomplish his divine plan (Mt. 16.21-23; Lk. 24.25-26; cf. Acts 2.23-24). For example, spirits designated as evil spirits (Judg. 9.23; 1 Sam. 16.14-16) and lying spirits (1 Kgs 22.19-23; 2 Chron. 18.18-22) became envoys of God.

They Fail to Understand the Role of Misfortunes in Life

In the Bible, God is occasionally presented as the source of misfortune, often as a punishment for sin. Some examples:
- 'The Lord brings death and makes alive...' (1 Sam. 2.6);
- the plagues on the Egyptians (Exodus 7–12);

- the affliction on the Philistines (1 Sam. 5.6-12);
- the striking of the seventy people of Beth Shemesh (1 Sam. 6.19-20);
- the death of Uzzah (2 Sam. 6.7);
- the sickness and death of David's child (2 Sam. 12.13-18);
- the muteness of Zechariah (Lk. 1.18-20);
- the death of Ananias and Sapphira (Acts 5.1-10);
- the blindness of Saul (Acts 9.8-9); the blindness of Elymas (Acts 13.8-12);
- and the death of Herod (Acts 12.21-23).

In other places, misfortunes can best be designated as 'neutral' or 'natural'. Some examples are:

- Isaac's blindness (Gen. 27.1);
- the death of the widow's son (1 Kgs 17.17-18);
- Elisha's sickness and subsequent death (2 Kgs 13.14);
- the death of eighteen people in Siloam (Lk. 13.4); and
- the illnesses of Paul's co-workers including Epaphroditus (Phil. 2.27), Timothy (1 Tim. 5.23), and Trophimus (2 Tim. 4.20).

The Bible does, however, recognize that some misfortunes originate from Satan (e.g. Job 1.6–2.10; 2 Cor. 12.7). But as I wrote earlier, Satan operates under God's sovereignty.

They Fail to Understand Satan's Operations

In the Bible, Satan's evils are his attempts to oppose God. In the Old Testament, Satan executes his plans on the people of God by hindering, inciting, or accusing them of moral evil as they carry out God's work (1 Chron. 21.1; Job 1–2; Zech. 3.1-2). Similarly, the main work of Satan and his demons in the New Testament is to oppose Christ and his Church (Mt. 4.1-12; 16.23; 1 Thess. 2.18).

Even when the Bible pictures the devil as attacking righteous people, Satan only carries out his plans with permission from God, and he works within that limitation (Job 1.12; Lk. 22.31; 2 Cor. 12.7-12; cf. 1 Cor. 10.13).

They Fail to Consider the Place of Suffering in Life

The biblical doctrine of the Fall teaches that suffering and death are part of life (Gen. 3.1-24; Rom. 5.12-14; 8.18-25). The whole human race fell as a result of the fall of Adam. Therefore, the whole of creation has 'been subjected to frustration'; that is, suffering and death exist as an inevitable part of the world. Yet creation has a hope of being 'liberated from its bondage to decay' (Rom. 8.18-24). The death and resurrection of Christ mark the beginning of the blessed hope, which means that 'God's final eschatological saving of his people has already been effected by Christ' (e.g. Eph. 1.7-10; 2.7). Believers, therefore, 'live between the times' of 'the already' but 'not yet' (e.g. Eph. 4.30; cf. Rom. 5.9; Gal. 5.5). The outcome of this eschatological tension is that Christians are still exposed to physical afflictions, suffering, and misfortunes. Misfortune does not necessarily mean that the devil has attacked; neither does it mean that the person has sinned. It may simply be the result of our fallen world.

They Reinforce the 'Primitive Animistic Belief System' that Hinders Progress and Keeps Communities and People in Servile Fearfulness

Sometimes, instead of trusting the power of God to deal with a situation while carrying on with preaching the Gospel, those engaged in spiritual warfare will spend a whole lot of time casting down strongholds or binding the strongman. For example, regarding poverty in Africa, spiritual warfare advocates often assign the blame to a spirit of poverty that hovers over the land, and they will travail for hours, and even days, to bind that spirit and render it powerless. In such situations, they may fail to address other factors such as laziness, indiscipline, and economic mismanagement, which continue to hamper our development. Moreover, in some instances people have blamed demons for the lack of progress in their villages – and they compound the problem by not putting up any more buildings in their hometowns.

They Fail to Address People's Sinfulness

When demons are associated with every vice, people are not forced to take responsibility for their wrongdoings, sins, and inadequacies. Instead they blame the devil or generational curses. The impression given by the advocates of spiritual warfare is that there are demons attached to all sinful intentions and behaviours. However, the Bible rarely speaks of demons as the source of sinful behaviours. Rather, Jesus taught that the heart is the source of sinful thoughts (e.g. Mt. 15.18-20; Mk 7.21-23). Similarly, Paul sees 'sin' as power in itself and the 'flesh' as that dimension of the Christian's personality where evil thoughts are manifested. Paul sets the flesh against the Spirit (Rom. 7.7-25; Gal. 5.19-22). Thus, it is 'the flesh' and not 'the demonic' that opposes the Spirit.

They Fail to Support it Biblically

Some spiritual warfare proponents admit that there is little biblical evidence for their teachings.[29] Because testimonies, rather than the Bible, have been the engine of this whole movement, charlatans have had the freedom to deceive people through their exaggerated stories, and they brand as sceptics anyone who challenges them. There is therefore the need to bring this to people's attention.

In view of the aforementioned, this book presents a fresh, biblical insight into spiritual warfare. This is the focus of the following chapters.

---

[29] Wagner, *Warfare Prayer*, pp. 19, 63.

PART TWO

REDEFINING THE WARFARE

4

IDENTIFYING THE WARFARE

In Part Two, we shall try to redefine the warfare as it is in the Bible. By doing this, we will be able to know the sort of weapons that we need for our Christian walk. We shall take some Bible readings to find out the nature of the warfare.

A Struggle (Ephesians 6.10-13)

The first scripture we shall consider is Eph. 6.10-13:

> Finally, be strong in the Lord and in his mighty power. Put on the full armour of God so that you can take your stand against the devil's schemes. For our struggle is not against flesh and blood, but against the rulers, against the authorities, against the powers of this dark world and against the spiritual forces of evil in the heavenly realms. Therefore put on the full armour of God, so that when the day of evil comes, you may be able to stand your ground, and after you have done everything, to stand (NIV).

Here Christians are instructed to be strong in the Lord and in His mighty power. Paul has spoken about the blessings of God to believers and the wisdom of God in working out His redemption for both Jews and Gentiles. The climax of God's purpose is to bring all things together in Christ who has been exalted above all. Christians must understand this in order to experience the blessings of God. Thus Paul prays for all believers and then ends his exhortation.

Paul's concern here is for Christians to understand the work of God and be strong in His mighty power. God's power already exists. Christians must know this and be strong in that power. How can they be strong? They must put on the whole armour of God in order to stand up against 'the devil's schemes' (Eph. 6.10-13). The point here is that the devil works with schemes. The New Living Translation is good for our purpose here, 'Put on all of God's armour so that you will be able to stand firm against all strategies and tricks of the Devil'. This shows that the devil uses strategies and tricks to work out his plan.

The person who uses tricks is the one who is able to deceive some people into believing that he is more powerful than he really is. Those who are good at using delusions and tricks are magicians. They do not have the power to kill and raise people, neither do they have the power to print new currency, yet they are able to use tricks to make it appear so. Magicians can often delude non-perceptive people into believing what is not real. Only strong people are able to stand.

Paul realises that this is how the devil works: Therefore, Christians need to put on the whole armour of God in order to stand against the devil's tricks. In order for Paul to explain his point well, he refers to a struggle – but not a war. 'For our struggle is not against flesh and blood but against the authorities ...' Here the word is not warfare but struggle or wrestle. Yet the term 'armour' used in the previous verse brings to mind a warfare picture. Nevertheless, the real issue here is not a battle between Christians and the devil, but a 'struggle', or a 'wrestle' as the King James Version puts it. What is the struggle?

The struggle here is the fundamental conflict between God and Satan, in which the human mind is the battleground. The real battle is between God and Satan. However, the North American pastor and Christian leader David Servant says, 'battle' is not the right word to describe the conflict between God and Satan. Because God is all powerful, he is not engaged in an actual battle. Servant prefers the term 'expulsion', because, as indicated in Lk. 10.17-18, when 'God decreed Satan's expulsion from heaven, *Satan could not resist.*'[30]

---

[30] David Servant, *The Disciple Making Minister: Biblical Principles for Fruitful and Multiplication* (Pittsburgh: Ethnos Press, 2005), pp. 385-86. The book is also available online at: www.shepherdserve.org/books/books.htm. Accessed: November

Servant's point is strong, because Satan cannot engage in real battle with God. However, for lack of a proper term, the word 'battle' will be used to describe the sort of contest that exists between Satan and the people of God from Genesis to Revelation. In each place, people's minds are the battleground. We see this in the Garden of Eden (Gen. 3.1-12), in the book of Job (1.6-22), in David's life (1 Chron. 21.1-2), and in the life of Joshua the High Priest (Zech. 3.1-4). On earth, Jesus had to go through this experience (e.g. Mt. 4.1-11). The battle comes to a climax in Revelation where the devil will exercise all his power against Christ and his kingdom:

> [7]And there was war in heaven: Michael and his angels fought against the dragon; and the dragon fought and his angels, [8]And prevailed not; neither was their place found any more in heaven. [9]And the great dragon was cast out, that old serpent, called the Devil, and Satan, which deceiveth the whole world: he was cast out into the earth, and his angels were cast out with him. [10]And I heard a loud voice saying in heaven, 'Now is come salvation, and strength, and the kingdom of our God, and the power of his Christ: for the accuser of our brethren is cast down, which accused them before our God day and night' (Rev. 12.7-10, KJV; see also Rev. 20.1-10).

In fact, in our own strength, we cannot fight with the devil; he will overpower us (Dan. 10.12-14; Zech. 3.1-3; 1 Pet. 5.8; 2 Pet. 2.11; Jude 8-10). Yet, the human being is involved in this conflict, since the human mind is the centre of this battle.

Paul explains that the devil uses all the powers of evil in the *heavenly realms* to carry out his schemes (Eph. 6.12). The King James Version puts it this way, 'For we wrestle ... against principalities, against powers, against the rulers of the darkness of this world, against spiritual wickedness in high places'. This means the devil does not work alone but with other evil forces to implement his plans. He does this through telling lies and accusing people. Jesus calls him the father of all lies (Jn 8.44). Through lies he is able to deceive a whole lot of people. In Rev. 12.7-10, for example, he is

---

21, 2007. Note that in some of the books, the name of this author is also written as David S. Kirkwood. When he was contacted on the email, he says, he prefers the name Servant. The problem that this poses is that you may not find the name 'Servant' on some of his printed books.

presented as leading the whole world astray and is also called the accuser (Rev. 12.7-10; 20.7-8). Accordingly, Paul ends the discourse by directing the believers to the available weapons for the warfare.

What we need to note in Eph. 6.10-13 is that Paul does not tell us the schemes of the devil nor the direct activities of what the devil and those principalities do. His real concern is for Christians to be strong in the Lord and in his mighty power in order to stand. The term 'stand' is used four times from verses 10-14. The implication here is that if people do not stand, they will be deceived by the devil. In order to stand, Paul shows the believers the weapons they have to use to win.

Warfare (2 Corinthians 10.3-6)

The next scripture to be considered is 2 Cor. 10.3-6:

> ³ For though we walk in the flesh, we do not war according to the flesh. ⁴ For the weapons of our warfare *are* not carnal but mighty in God for pulling down strongholds, ⁵ casting down arguments and every high thing that exalts itself against the knowledge of God, bringing every thought into captivity to the obedience of Christ, ⁶ and being ready to punish all disobedience when your obedience is fulfilled (NKJV).

The passage indicates that we are in warfare. We are human, but we don't wage war with human plans and methods. When Paul says that we live 'in the flesh', he means we are human beings. 'We do not war after the flesh' means we do not wage war with human plans and strength. Paul continues by telling us that our weapons are powerful enough to destroy strongholds. He does not tell us the nature of the weapons, as he did in Ephesians, but he has informed us that the weapons are strong enough to demolish strongholds. Thus, here, the warfare has been identified as strongholds.

The strongholds are described to enable us to understand what they mean. They are ideas, beliefs, arguments, and philosophies that make people disobedient to God and keep them from knowing him. The warfare here is therefore not a direct battle against the devil with human strength, but against the devil's strongholds of belief systems. These are the devil's schemes. We need the weapons that have divine power to demolish them. The weapons, however, have not been described.

The Fight of Faith (1 Timothy 1.18-20; 6.12)

The third Scripture to consider is 1 Tim. 1.18-20; 6.12:

> Timothy, my son, here are my instructions for you, based on the prophetic words spoken about you earlier. May they give you the confidence to fight well in the Lord's battles. Cling tightly to your faith in Christ, and always keep your conscience clear. For some people have deliberately violated their consciences; as a result, their faith has been shipwrecked. Hymenaeus and Alexander are two examples of this. I turned them over to Satan so they would learn not to blaspheme God (1.18-20, NLT).

> Fight the good fight of faith, lay hold on eternal life, whereunto thou art also called, and hast professed a good profession before many witnesses (6.12 KJV).

The struggle or warfare has been identified as the Lord's battle, or good fight of faith. What is Paul asking Timothy to fight for? He had already made himself clear in his first letter to Tim. in 1.3-7.

> [3] When I left for Macedonia, I urged you to stay there in Ephesus and stop those who are teaching wrong doctrine. [4] Don't let people waste time in endless speculation over myths and spiritual pedigrees. For these things only cause arguments; they don't help people live a life of faith in God. [5] The purpose of my instruction is that all the Christians there would be filled with love that comes from a pure heart, a clear conscience, and sincere faith. [6] But some teachers have missed this whole point. They have turned away from these things and spend their time arguing and talking foolishness. [7] They want to be known as teachers of the law of Moses, but they don't know what they are talking about, even though they seem so confident (NLT).

The fight of faith is a fight against false teachings. Two areas of false teachings can be identified here, and in 1 Tim. 4.1-2, Paul clearly explains the sources of false teaching,

Now the Holy Spirit tells us clearly that in the last times some will turn away from what we believe; they will follow lying spirits and teachings that come from demons. These teachers are hypocrites and liars. They pretend to be religious, but their consciences are dead (NLT).

The sources, he identifies, are deceiving spirits and demons. This means the deceiving spirits will use lies to deceive believers about their faith in Christ to turn them against God.

Therefore, by saying 'fight the good fight of faith', Paul wants Timothy to:

Command certain men not to teach false doctrine nor **waste time in** myths (1 Tim. 1.3-7). This means Timothy should not, as a leader, tolerate people who teach false doctrines and myths. He should stop them.

Point out the truth to the Christians (1 Tim. 4.6-7; 11-14). He should teach the true and simple message of the gospel. The message of the gospel should be preached in season and out of season.

Guard what has been entrusted to his care (1 Tim. 6.3-5, 20-21; 2 Tim. 1.14). He should hold on to what has been given to him. The message that has been passed on to him is the true gospel. He should not be interested in speculation and myths.

This is the fight of faith – commanding or stopping people from teaching false doctrine, pointing out the simple and true gospel to people, and guarding that which has been entrusted to you.

Summary

What is the battle or the warfare we are engaged in as Christians? We have discovered that there is 'warfare' but the real issue is between God and Satan. Ephesians calls it a struggle, 1 Corinthians labels it as warfare, and 1 Timothy identifies it as the fight of faith. Ephesians mentions the struggle but it does not define it. However, we learn the weapons that we need for our victory. 1 Corinthians informs us that the weapons of our warfare are not carnal, but it does not explain the nature of the weapons. Nevertheless, we learn the type of warfare that in which we are engaged: these are false ideas, arguments, and beliefs. The warfare idea is further described as false teaching in 1 Timothy. The charge for the soldiers of Christ is to preach the simple and true gospel to people, and guard that which has been entrusted to them.

We can have the full grasp of what Paul intends to tell believers when we bring together the three passages. There is some opposition going on against God by Satan. We, as human beings, are directly involved in this 'battle' because our minds are the battleground. Our involvement is described by Paul as the 'struggle', 'wrestle', 'warfare', or 'fight of faith'. The scheme of the devil is to use his evil powers in the heavenly realms to plant strongholds in the form of false doctrines, beliefs, and ideologies in people. These are so strong that we need to put on the whole armour of God to stand, and we tear them down by preaching the Word.

We turn to the next chapter to find out the victories that have been won for Christians in the warfare.

5

THE VICTORIES OF JESUS

The 'battle' is between God and Satan. The Lord Jesus has already defeated Satan and all his evil powers. He did that through his ministry on earth, his death on the cross, and his triumphant resurrection.

1. Jesus Defeated Satan on His Own Behalf at the Wilderness Temptation

The wilderness temptation is sometimes not considered very important in the ministry of Christ. Nevertheless, it is very important because if Christ had failed as the last Adam, humanity would have been without hope. The question that may be asked is, Could he have failed? Well, if he could not have failed then Jesus was never seriously tempted. Because he did not only come as the Son of God, but also as the Son of Man, the possibility of failure was real. The importance of the temptation and his victory is what we now examine. Matthew 4.1-11:

> [1] Then Jesus was led out into the wilderness by the Holy Spirit to be tempted there by the Devil. [2] For forty days and forty nights he ate nothing and became very hungry. [3] Then the Devil came and said to him, 'If you are the Son of God, change these stones into loaves of bread.' [4] But Jesus told him, 'No! The Scriptures say, "People need more than bread for their life; they must feed on every word of God"'. [5] Then the Devil took him to Jerusalem, to the highest point of the Temple, [6] and said, 'If you are the Son of God, jump off! For the Scriptures say, "He orders his angels

to protect you. And they will hold you with their hands to keep you from striking your foot on a stone"'. [7] Jesus responded, 'The Scriptures also say, "Do not test the Lord your God"'. [8] Next the Devil took him to the peak of a very high mountain and showed him the nations of the world and all their glory. [9] 'I will give it all to you', he said, 'if you will only kneel down and worship me'. [10] 'Get out of here, Satan', Jesus told him. 'For the Scriptures say, "You must worship the Lord your God; serve only him"'. [11] Then the Devil went away, and angels came and cared for Jesus (NLT).

Here Jesus was tempted as the last Adam. His victory marked the beginning of the defeat of Satan on earth. The temptation of Jesus was significant. The devil tempted the first Adam, who was also the first human being, and won the battle. When he tempted Jesus, his aim was to divert him from the cross, that is, to lure him from obedience to the will of God. The cross was the plan of God to redeem humanity from sin.

The temptation came in three ways. First, he wanted Jesus to gratify the flesh. This is self-gratification. 'Then the Devil came and said to him, "If you are the Son of God, change these stones into loaves of bread"' (Mt. 4.3 NLT). Jesus was hungry, and the devil wanted him to satisfy that desire. Satisfaction of the flesh is one of the devil's greatest temptations. The first Adam failed here. He saw that the tree was good for food and he could not resist (Gen. 3.6). Jesus was victorious in the sense that he resisted the desire to satisfy the flesh, 'No! The Scriptures say, "People need more than bread for their life; they must feed on every word of God"' (Mt. 4.4).

The second temptation was geared toward public display. 'If you are the Son of God, jump off! For the Scriptures say, "He orders his angels to protect you. And they will hold you with their hands to keep you from striking your foot on a stone"' (Mt. 4.6). This temptation offered glamour and thrill. There was a myth that the Messiah would come from heaven. An injury-free leap from the pinnacle of the Temple would have proved to the people that he was the Messiah – though a cheap Messiah, a Messiah without the cross. It was also dangerous, because tempting God that way could have cost his life.

The third temptation was geared toward self-glorification and false worship. Here the devil wanted to use worldliness to attract the Messiah. Satan wanted Jesus to worship him, avoid the cross, and gain riches and glory. This temptation was the lust of the eye. 'The Devil took him to the peak of a very high mountain and showed him the nations of the world and all their glory. "I will give it all to you", he said, "if you will only kneel down and worship me"' (Mt. 4.8-9, NLT). Here again, Jesus commanded Satan to get out, and referred him to the Scripture which says, you must worship the Lord God alone.

Take notice that in defeating Satan Jesus used the Word of God. Jesus had fasted and prayed but the devil came to tempt him. Paul says that 'and after you have done everything to stand' (Eph. 6.13). This is where many Christians fail. They do not stand when they face problems and challenges. The evil day will by all means come, but you need to stand. Jesus used the armour of God. He used the Word of God throughout the temptation to overcome Satan. I can't overemphasise the importance of the Word of God. Even when the devil used the Word of God wrongly, Jesus answered, 'It is also written "Do not put the Lord your God to the test"' (Mt. 4.7). The devil knows the Word of God and can misquote it to you. You need to stand your ground.

When Jesus finally commanded the devil to leave, Luke reports that he only left him until another opportunity came (Lk. 4.13; cf. Mt. 4.11). In other words, God allowed Jesus to be tempted repeatedly. Throughout the ministry of Jesus, the devil continued to tempt him by working through the people around him (Jn 13.27). One of the lessons we learn here is that you can never permanently drive the devil away, but you can overcome him by the Word of God.

Jesus' Life was Satan's Death
The devil continued to oppose the earthly ministry of our Lord Jesus, but the gospels show that Jesus triumphed over him. The gospels teach that the Messianic age had begun, the kingdom of God had broken into human history, and it was powerfully displacing demons and healing diseases. The numerous summary statements throughout the gospels about the healings and exorcisms of Jesus (e.g. Mt. 4.23-24; 9.35; Mk 1.39; Lk. 6.18-19) are often summed up under the call to repentance 'for the kingdom of God is near' (Mk 1.15). Thus the Messiah was inaugurating the kingdom of God in

power. The power to heal and cast out demons demonstrated the inauguration.[31]

Jesus summarised his activities to Herod, 'Go tell that fox, "I will drive out demons and heal people today and tomorrow, and the third day I will reach my goal"' (Lk. 13.32, NIV). The eschatological Jubilee was proclaimed, announcing liberty from bondage to sin, Satan and sickness (Lk. 4.18-19). Thus, the mission of Jesus was directly linked with his power demonstrated in the casting out of demons and the healing of diseases.

As Jesus taught at a synagogue in Capernaum, a man possessed by an evil spirit cried, 'What do you want with us, Jesus of Nazareth? Have you come to destroy us? I know who you are – the Holy One of God!' (Mk 1.24, NIV). The demons recognised the person as well as the mission of Jesus. They knew Jesus was the Holy One of God, and they knew His purpose was to destroy them.

Jesus' Disciples Live in Two Worlds

In an exchange with the Pharisees, Jesus declared, 'If I drive demons by the Spirit of God then the kingdom of God has come to you' (Mt. 12.28). The exorcisms of Jesus demonstrated the inauguration of the kingdom of God that was powerfully clashing with, and visibly breaking into, the kingdom of Satan. Consequently, the supernatural ministry of Jesus announced the inauguration of the kingdom. The Kingdom of God was inaugurated by Jesus, but it has not yet been consummated, because the present world has not yet passed away. The two ages co-exist. These ages are **the present world** and **the kingdom of God** that was inaugurated by Jesus. We Christians live in both ages. This situation will continue until the Second Coming of our Lord Jesus Christ. Jesus recognized this reality when he prayed, 'I have given them your word and the world hated them, for they are not of the world anymore than I am of the world. My prayer is not that you take them out of the world but that you protect them from the evil one. They are not of the world, even as I am not of it' (Jn 17.14-16, NIV). Jesus was praying that the Lord would protect his people from the evil one in the world in which they live. Although they live in the world, they are not of the world.

---

[31] Opoku Onyinah, 'Matthew Speaks to Ghanaian Healing Situations', *Journal of Pentecostal Theology* 10.1 (2001), pp. 120-43.

Christians live within these worlds. Although Jesus inaugurated the age to come, we still live in this present world dominated by Satan.

2. Jesus Defeated Satan on the Cross on Our Behalf

Jesus' death on the cross was the devil's defeat. The power of Satan over human beings was based on sin. The death of Jesus as an atonement for sin means the power of Satan has been broken. The New Testament addresses this in diverse ways.

Jesus' Death Was Satan's Defeat

Satan held people captive because of sin. He is the father of all sinners. The death of Jesus which atoned for sin broke Satan's hold on humanity. One of the key passages is Col. 2.12-15:

> For you were buried with Christ when you were baptized. And with him you were raised to a new life because you trusted the mighty power of God, who raised Christ from the dead. You were dead because of your sins and because your sinful nature was not yet cut away. Then God made you alive with Christ. He forgave all our sins. He cancelled the record that contained the charges against us. He took it and destroyed it by nailing it to Christ's cross. In this way, God disarmed the evil rulers and authorities. He shamed them publicly by his victory over them on the cross of Christ (NLT).

Here Paul shows the power of the cross over sin and Satan. First, he explains that sin has been dealt with, and forgiveness of sin is granted to those who are in Christ. Then, he shows that Christ has disarmed Satan by his death on the cross. Keith Ferdinando rightly articulates that 'it is precisely by addressing the problem of sin that Christ's atoning work also, in consequence, brings about the defeat of Satan and the powers'.[32] Consequently in Col. 2.15, the disarmament and public spectacle of the powers and authorities follow the cancellation of the written code against sinners.

---

[32] Keith Ferdinando, 'Sickness and Syncretism in the African Context', in *Mission and Meaning: Essays Presented to Peter Cotterell* (eds. Anthony Billington, et. al.; Carlisle: Paternoster, 1995), p. 281. See also Keith Ferdinando, *The Triumph of Christ in African Perspective: A Study of Demonology and Redemption in the African Concept* (Carlisle: Paternoster, 1999).

In Gal. 1.4, for example, 'He died for our sins, just as God our Father planned, in order to rescue us from this evil world in which we live'. That is, the purpose of Jesus dying for our sins was to rescue human beings from this evil world dominated by Satan (cf. 2 Cor. 4.4). By this Paul, like Jesus, divided the history of the world into two: this present, evil world in which we live and the age to come. Ephesians 1.21 brings this into sharper focus, 'Now he is far above any ruler or authority or power or leader or anything else in this world or in the world to come'. The world to come or the age to come (as the NIV translates it) was inaugurated by Jesus when he came on earth (Mt. 12.32; Mk 10.30).[33] However, because the present age has not passed away, the two ages are running side by side. Jesus' death was to rescue us from the power of the present age and transfer us into the power of the age to come. We have not yet reached the new age, but we have begun to experience its reality. Jesus' death has given us the power to live the life of the coming age in this present age.

In Acts 26.15-19, where Paul recounted his encounter with Christ, he made it clear that God commissioned him to preach so that all would turn from their sins, receive forgiveness of sins, and be delivered from Satan's power.

> 'Who are you, sir?' I asked. And the Lord replied, 'I am Jesus, the one you are persecuting. Now stand up! For I have appeared to you to appoint you as my servant and my witness. You are to tell the world about this experience and about other times I will appear to you. And I will protect you from both your own people and the Gentiles. Yes, I am going to send you to the Gentiles, to open their eyes so they may turn from darkness to light, and from the power of Satan to God. Then they will receive forgiveness for their sins and be given a place among God's people, who are set apart by faith in me.' And so, O King Agrippa, I was not disobedient to that vision from heaven. I preached first to those in Damascus, then in Jerusalem and throughout all Judea, and also to the Gentiles, that all must turn from their sins and turn to God – and prove they have changed by the good things they do. (NLT).

---

[33] This has been discussed at point 1 of this chapter.

The forgiveness of sin is connected to deliverance from Satan. Put another way, to turn away from the power of darkness, which is Satan, is to be placed in the light of God, which is the kingdom of God.

Other New Testament passages also suggest that forgiveness of sins, as an aspect of salvation, is linked with deliverance from the powers of the evil one (e.g. Col. 1.13-14; Heb. 2.14-18, 1 Jn 3.8; Rev. 12.7-12).

Through the death of Christ, Satan's main weapon has been broken. In fact once a person receives Jesus into his/her life, the divine exchange takes place. God no longer counts the person's sins against him/her. The person's sins are forgiven and he/she becomes the righteousness of God. 2 Corinthians emphasises this, 'For he hath made him to be sin for us, who knew no sin; that we might be made the righteousness of God in him' (2 Cor. 5.21, KJV). Once we understand that we have been made right with God through the death of Christ, Satan's power is genuinely weakened.

The point that we have digested through these texts is that our Lord Jesus Christ has defeated Satan and his evil powers through his death on the cross, which was a death to sin (Rom. 6.10). Believers share in Christ's victory through faith in him. Therefore, Satan and his evil powers do not have control or power over believers.

The Church Declares God's Wisdom to Satan's Realm

After God had forgiven our sin and delivered us from the dominion of Satan, he reconciled both Jews and Gentiles in Christ to become his (God's) dwelling place.

> By his death he ended the whole system of Jewish law that excluded the Gentiles. His purpose was to make peace between Jews and Gentiles by creating in himself one new person from the two groups. Together as one body, Christ reconciled both groups to God by means of his death, and our hostility toward each other was put to death (Eph. 2.15-16, NLT).

> We who believe are carefully joined together, becoming a holy temple for the Lord. Through him you Gentiles are also joined together as part of this dwelling where God lives by his Spirit (Eph. 2.21-22, NLT).

His dwelling place which he inhabits by his Spirit is called the Church (Eph. 3.6-11). That God was to place both Jews and Gentiles on an equal level was not clearly revealed in Old Testament times. This act of God, the establishment of the Church in which Jews and Gentiles are equal, is the best place for God to demonstrate his wisdom to all. His wisdom was to be explained to everyone (Eph. 3.9) and also to the rulers and authorities in heavenly realms (Eph. 3.10):

> [6] And this is the secret plan: The Gentiles have an equal share with the Jews in all the riches inherited by God's children. Both groups have believed the Good News, and both are part of the same body and enjoy together the promise of blessings through Christ Jesus. [7] By God's special favour and mighty power, I have been given the wonderful privilege of serving him by spreading this Good News.[8] Just think! Though I did nothing to deserve it, and though I am the least deserving Christian there is, I was chosen for this special joy of telling the Gentiles about the endless treasures available to them in Christ. [9] I was chosen to explain to *everyone* this plan that God, the Creator of all things, had kept secret from the beginning. [10] God's purpose was to show his wisdom in all its rich variety to *all the rulers and authorities in the heavenly realms*. They will see this when Jews and Gentiles are joined together in his church. [11] This was his plan from all eternity, and it has now been carried out through Christ Jesus our Lord. [12] Because of Christ and our faith in him, we can now come fearlessly into God's presence, assured of his glad welcome. (Eph. 3.6-12, NLT, Italics mine).

Paul explains that the great power of God was also available to Gentiles, who were afraid of demonic powers, and he allayed their fears. First, in 1.21, Paul shows that Christ has been exalted above all rulers and powers in the heavenly realms, then in 2.6-7, he wrote that God raised believers with Christ in the heavenly realms above all these powers. Then, in 3.6-11, he showed that God demonstrates his wisdom, through the body of believers called the Church. Satan and his evil forces now exist as witnesses to what God has done and is doing through his body of believers. This is why in 6.13 Paul says we struggle against these powers. They envy what God has done for human beings in Christ.[34]

As a result of what God has done, we believers, can enter God's presence with confidence. 'Because of Christ and our faith in him, we can now come fearlessly into God's presence, assured of his glad welcome' (Eph. 3.12). We do not go there as foreigners who are pleading our case, but as sons who have the right of inheritance through the blood of Jesus to both God's throne and his properties. The book of Hebrews clarifies this:

> And so, dear brothers and sisters, we can boldly enter heaven's Most Holy Place because of the blood of Jesus. This is the new, life-giving way that Christ has opened up for us through the sacred curtain, by means of his death for us. And since we have a great High Priest who rules over God's people, let us go right into the presence of God, with true hearts fully trusting him. For our evil consciences have been sprinkled with Christ's blood to make us clean, and our bodies have been washed with pure water. Without wavering, let us hold tightly to the hope we say we have, for God can be trusted to keep his promise (10.19-23, NLT).

The heavenly Most Holy Place is above the evil powers. Christians have the authority to go there and ask whatsoever they want.

Christ's Resurrection was His Victory and Ours

The resurrection announces Christ's victory to both humanity and spiritual powers, be they angels or demons, and it allows Christ to apply his victory to us. Paul says, 'If Christ has not been raised, our preaching is useless and so is our faith' (1 Cor. 15.14, NIV). The authority of Christ is based on his resurrection. The benefits of the resurrection are beyond the cross. These benefits affect our daily walk with him and our legal position; we are living in the heavenly realms. At the resurrection of Christ, believers received a standing in the heavenly realms. 'For he raised us from the dead along with Christ, and we are seated with him in the heavenly realms – all because we are one with Christ Jesus' (Eph. 2.6). We are now in union

---

[34] Arthur G. Patzia, *New International Biblical Commentary*, 'Ephesians, Colossians, Philemon' (Peabody: Hendrickson, 1990), pp. 213-17.

with Christ and work together with him (e.g. Rom. 6.5; 8.17; 2 Cor. 6.1; Col. 2.13; 1 Thess. 5.10; Rom. 8.17).

The resurrection has therefore imparted power to believers, which many do not understand. Therefore, Paul prayed:

> I pray that you will begin to understand the incredible greatness of his power for us who believe him. This is the same mighty power that raised Christ from the dead and seated him in the place of honour at God's right hand in the heavenly realms. Now he is far above any ruler or authority or power or leader or anything else in this world or in the world to come (Eph. 1.19-21, NLT).

The power of God in the believer is mighty and is the same power that raised Jesus from death and seated him at God's right hand in the heavenly realms. Christ's resurrection signals the devil's defeat. Believers have been assured several times in Ephesians that we have been placed in Christ who is above all powers and authorities.[35] Some Christians behave as if there were no power in the cross and in the resurrection of Christ. If all believers would understand and appropriate Christ's victory, they would live and work more effectively. Believers must not live defeated lives. God's unlimited power has been invested in us. Satan and the evil forces know about it, but sometimes believers do not. Elmer Towns declares, 'This accomplishment of Calvary wins God's approval for us; the resurrection of Christ announces it to the world.'[36]

3. The Responsibility of the Believer

The responsibility of Christians is to appropriate and administer Jesus' victory in our lives. Many Christians are unable to apply Christ's victories in their daily lives. Through Christ's death and resurrection we have received eternal life, been made the righteousness of God, defeated the devil and his powers, and are more than conquerors. This is our standing, position or status – and it is who we are and the power we have. Our present experience, however,

---

[35] In Christ and seated with him in the heavenly realms occur about 93 times in the book, 89 times in Greek.

[36] Elmer L. Towns, *What the Faith is All About: A Study of the Basic Doctrines of Christianity* (Wheaton: Tyndale House Publishers, 1983), p. 201.

may be different. In other words, there may be a difference between what we should be and who we are. Once we received Christ into our life in faith, we received all the benefits of salvation. Yet, although we possess these benefits in status, we may not be permitting Christ to exhibit his power in us. Or, our life in this present world may be filled with struggles and temptations which we may have to strive to overcome. This is where we need to apply the victory of Christ.

To put it another way, as a Christian, your responsibility is to apply the work of Christ in your Christian life. God will not do that for you. You will have to accept it by faith and apply it by faith. Paul clearly explains in Rom. 1.17, 'This Good News tells us how God makes us right in his sight. This is accomplished from start to finish by faith. As the Scriptures say, "It is through faith that a righteous person has life."' The Christian message is received by faith. Therefore, you will have to apply what God has done for you in Christ by faith. God cannot do this for you.

When it comes to overcoming the power of Satan in your life, you must accept what God has said. For example, Col. 2.15 tells us that Christ disarmed Satan and his evil forces and made a public show of them by triumphing over them by the cross. God works this victory in our lives as we accept and apply it. In 2 Corinthians 2.14, Paul wrote that wherever we go, God leads us in Christ's triumphal procession: 'But thanks be to God, who made us his captives and leads us along in Christ's triumphal procession. Now wherever we go he uses us to tell others about the Lord and to spread the Good News like a sweet perfume' (2 Cor. 2.14, NLT).

Triumphal procession is not the winning of the victory but the celebration of the victory. Jesus has won the battle for us already, but we need to apply it in our lives. The good news here is that, as the NIV puts it, 'God always leads us' (2 Cor. 2.14, NIV) in Christ's triumphal victory against the devil over his kingdom. He does this in every place. Thus, God will always lead us everywhere to walk in Christ's victory over Satan and his evil forces. The problem lies with our lack of understanding regarding this important truth. Once we believe it and walk in it, God will always honour His Word.

The devil will apply all his schemes to keep people from God's grace or, at least, let people feel that God's love or the incomparable riches of his grace are received through human efforts.

This leads us to the next chapters, where we will learn the devil's ways of blocking people from knowing God's provision for them.

We learned in this chapter that Jesus Christ has already defeated Satan. He did that through his ministry on earth, his death on the cross, and his triumphant resurrection. In the wilderness encounter with Satan, Jesus defeated Satan as the last Adam. During His earthly ministry, Jesus' expulsion of demons was also a demonstration of his victory over Satan: the kingdom of God was breaking through the satanic kingdom, and satanic powers could not withstand it.

Through the death of Jesus, Satan's grip on humanity through the power of sin was broken, and the resurrection of Jesus allows him to apply all of His victories to believers.

After God had forgiven our sin and delivered us from the dominion of Satan, He reconciled both Jews and Gentiles in Christ to become His (God's) dwelling place, which is the Church. Through the Church God demonstrates His wisdom to the world as we look forward to the world to come. This means that all Christians live in two worlds: this world while tasting of the next. Why? The kingdom of God was inaugurated by Jesus, but this kingdom has not been consummated because the present world has not yet passed away. The consequence is that the two ages (the present world and the kingdom of God) co-exist. Christians live within these two ages. This situation will continue until the Second Coming of our Lord Jesus Christ.

The aspect of Jesus' work that many Christians find difficult to accept or implement is the application of his victories in their daily lives. The responsibility of Christians is to appropriate and also administer the victory of Jesus in their lives through faith.

PART THREE

THE DEVIL'S SCHEME: STRONGHOLDS

6

STRONGHOLD 1: FALSE DOCTRINES

Strongholds: Introduction

We have learned that the battle is between God and Satan, and that Satan has been defeated. Jesus accomplished this through his ministry on earth, his death on the cross, and his triumphant resurrection. Our responsibility as Christians is to apply Jesus' victory into our daily lives.

The devil's schemes are his efforts to block us from knowing Christ's victories, and especially what he has done for human beings. The following chapters, 6-13, describe those schemes, strategies, and tricks.

We discovered in 2 Cor. 10.3-5 that the Christian is engaged in warfare against the devil's 'strongholds'. Strongholds are arguments, pretensions, false philosophies, beliefs, doctrines, teachings, and practices which result in arrogance and rebellion against the gospel of our Lord Jesus Christ (2 Cor. 10.5; Eph. 2.1-4). The reason the devil operates this way is that he knows he is defeated and the battle has been lost. But if he is able to deceive people to believe and behave according to false doctrines and ideas, he can get people to his side. Some examples of these are needed for our understanding.

Why are they considered 'strongholds'? A false ideology is attractive enough to be believed and not easily removed once a person grabs onto it. When people wrap their lives around a certain belief or worldview, you can't easily get them to change their thinking. The ideology that a person follows has a 'strong hold' on him or her. A person who believes that Joseph Smith, the founder of the

Church of Jesus Christ of Latter Days Saints, is a messenger of God will not be easily convinced otherwise. His or her mind is anchored to Mormonism, and dislodging that doctrine requires the Spirit of God.

The false ideas, beliefs, and teachings that shape many people's lives are attractive enough to believe and not easily removed. The devil implants them firmly. That's why we need the armour of God – to resist them from entering our own minds and to assist in removing them from others'.

False Doctrines in the Church

As already stated, strongholds are false teachings, but we will start with those in the Church.

Believers Who Wander Away from the Truth

One of the strongholds or the weapons that the devil uses to attack the Church is false doctrines or 'heresies'. False teachers usually take one element of truth and blow it out of proportion. Some false teachers begin their Christian life genuinely in Christ and have good intentions. Unfortunately, because of misguided opinions, poor biblical understanding or sin (such as pride, immorality, or love of money), their personal commitment to Christ fades; they wander away from the truth (Acts 20.29-31; 2 Tim. 2.16-19; 4.10; 2 Pet. 2.1-3). Paul refers to 'false apostles who disguise themselves as apostles of Christ, just as Satan disguises himself as an angel of light' (2 Cor. 11.13-15). This type of enemy has been destroying Christianity more than any other one. Fritz Ridenour observes, 'Christianity has always had its foes, but no enemy has been more dangerous than the enemy "within" – those who hold opinion in opposition to the commonly received truths on which Christianity was founded.'[37]

Those Who Have Never Been Believers

Other false teachers have never been genuine believers in Christ at all. They come to the church with evil motives and deceive through various means. They neglect certain basic scriptures and twist others to support the point that they are trying to teach. David Servant

---

[37] Fritz Ridenour, *So What's the Difference?* (Ventura: Regal Books, 1979), pp. 9-10.

calls such teaching 'foreign grace'.[38] They do this cunningly and mislead followers of the truth for their selfish gain.

Such people may be planted in the church by Satan (Mt. 13.24-30, 36-43; 2 Thess. 2.3-12; 2 Pet. 3.3-7). Satan uses such people's abilities and charisma, and he helps them to succeed. His purpose is to place them in influential positions in order to undermine the work of Christ. If such people are not exposed, Satan will use them to shame the work of Christ.

Examples of False Doctrines

The purpose of this book is not to explore all the false teachings that encompass our world, but I will touch on a couple that immediately impact the spiritual warfare movement in Ghana.

Most false teachings misrepresent the person of Christ. One ancient teaching with modern repercussions is Docetism, which teaches that Jesus was divine but only appeared to be human because God would never suffer. John's letters refute this doctrine (1 Jn 1.1; 4.2; 2 Jn 7).

Docetism is actually a form of Gnosticism, a heresy that became a full-blown problem for the Church in the second century. Gnosticism insisted that the body and the physical world were evil and secret knowledge was the source of salvation. Like Docetism, it taught that Christ only appeared to be human. However, orthodox Christianity insists that Jesus was fully human and fully God.

Marcion was a second-century heretic who held to many Gnostic-like teachings. He propounded that the God of the Old Testament was completely different from the God of the New Testament. He rejected the Old Testament and issued his own New Testament, which contained only part of Luke and only ten of Paul's letters. God used him for good, however, because he motivated the early Church to think seriously about the New Testament canon.[39]

Why should we care about Docetism? Because it still exists today. A modern-day example is Christian Science. 'Mary Baker Eddy taught that the entire material world is unreal, and that suffering is

---

[38] David Servant, *The Great Gospel Deception: Exposing the False Promise of Heaven Without Holiness* (Pittsburgh: Ethnos Press, 1999), p. 164.
[39] 'Marcion', *New International Dictionary of the Christian Church*, 2nd (ed., J.D. Douglas, ed.; Grand Rapids: Zondervan, 1978), pp. 629-30.

illusory and only appears to exist due to the absence of faith.'[40] Many deliverance services also exhibit docetic tendencies when they try to drive away all forms of suffering from believers' lives. Docetism is not just an ancient heresy but still fights for our attention today.

Another ancient heresy that we still feel today is Arianism, which teaches that Jesus was neither fully human nor fully God; he was a lesser god. Modern-day Jehovah's Witnesses continue this heresy today, and this stronghold in their mind is very difficult to break.

Apollinarianism was a misguided attempt in the early Church to explain how Jesus was both God and man. It taught that Christ had a human body but not a human soul because his soul was the dwelling of God. That heresy undermines the truth that Jesus was fully human. A form of this teaching arises in deliverance services with their repeated invoking of the 'blood of Jesus', as if Jesus' blood had some magical quality. Jesus' blood, however, was human blood. In Scripture, references to Jesus' blood are simply 'a vivid way of saying that we owe our salvation to the death of Christ'.[41]

These heresies all arose in the first few centuries of the early Church. Other heresies could be mentioned, but what is important is that heresies never die but continue to manifest themselves today. They pose significant problems for the church by damaging faith and causing divisions. We should be aware of them so that we don't succumb to their seductive appeals.

How to Identify False Teaching

The greatest question that we can ask is, How can the Church identify false teaching? Generally, to identify false teachings is to compare the teachings of a group of people with the teachings in the Bible. God's truth never contradicts itself. God's revelation has been progressive within the Bible. There are some things that God did not reveal straightaway. But as Robert Bowman rightly states, 'Later truth never contradicts earlier truth, but it may supplement it

---

[40] C. FitzSimons Allison, *The Cruelty of Heresy* (London: SPCK, 1994), p. 30.
[41] L. Morris, 'Blood', *Evangelical Dictionary of Theology* (Walter Elwell, ed.; Grand Rapids: Baker Books, 2001), p. 176.

or complete it; and later commands may replace earlier ones.'[42] If the teachings of a group are contrary to God's Word, the group is either teaching heresy or heading toward it.

False teachings often stress human-made rules, and observing rituals and taboos rather than receiving God's grace. They foster a critical spirit toward the simplicity of the word of God. They stress formulas, secret knowledge, or special visions more than the word of God. Rather than elevating Christ, they elevate self-righteousness and honour those who keep the rules.

False teachers also neglect Christ's universal church and claim that they and their followers are an elite or a selected group. The late Walter Martin, who studied the cults, wrote, 'Almost without exception, all cultic belief systems manifest a type of institutional dogmatism and a pronounced intolerance for any position but their own.'[43] This, they claim, is supernaturally given. They teach that their way is the only way to peace and happiness.

Jesus points out the real test, 'You can detect them by the way they act, just as you can identify a tree by its fruit' (Mt. 7.16, NLT). False teaching is one of the devil's greatest weapons against Christianity. Beware of it.

---

[42] Robert M. Bowman, Jr., *Understanding Jehovah's Witnesses: Why They Read the Bible the Way They Do* (Grand Rapids: Baker Book, 1991), p. 36.
[43] Walter Martin, The *Kingdom of the Cults* (ed. Hank Hanegraaff; Minneapolis: Bethany House Publishers, 2003), p. 38.

7

STRONGHOLD 2: THE FLESH

The Nature of Satan and Demonic Opposition to Christians

The work of Satan and the powers is to convince us to live for ourselves rather than for God. To achieve their intentions, they seek to influence Christians to live in ways which are contrary to the Word of God.

For example, in the Old Testament, Satan encouraged Eve to break God's command (Gen. 3.1-6), he tempted Job to forsake God (Job 1–2), he misled David (1 Chron. 21.1), and accused Joshua the High Priest (Zech. 3.1-2). In Luke, he had evil designs for Peter (Lk. 22.31-34, 55-62).

In each of those cases, and in our own lives as well, Satan tries to turn us against ourselves. That is, he appeals for us to use our bodies and our minds in wrong ways. The Bible calls that 'walking according to the flesh' (Rom. 8.13). The flesh of our bodies is of course not sinful; it's our skin and serves to protect our muscles, bones, and organs. But the Bible also uses the word 'flesh' in a negative way. Living according to the flesh is when we live for our own pleasures and purposes rather than for the pleasures and purposes of God. Living according to the flesh is directly opposed to living according to the Spirit.[44]

---

[44] For more on how to overcome the flesh see, Opoku Onyinah, *Are Two Persons the Same: How to Overcome your Weaknesses in Temperament* (Accra, Ghana: Pentecost Press Ltd, 2004).

Flesh against the Spirit, Not against the Demonic

The New Testament urges Christians not to yield to the cravings of the flesh and thus allow sin to have dominion in their lives (Rom. 6.12; Col. 3: 5; Heb. 12.14-17; Jas 4.1-10; 1 Pet. 1.15-21; cf. 1 Jn 3.2-6). Paul especially recognises that although the compelling influence of the flesh has been broken by the work of Christ, the inner compulsion continually seeks to reassert its claim on Christians. He provides several lists of categories of sins, but in all of these he does not contrast 'the flesh' with 'the demonic', but rather with the 'new man' or 'the Spirit' (e.g. 1 Cor. 5.11; 6.9-10; 2 Cor. 12.20; Gal. 5.19-23; Eph. 4.17-24; Col. 3: 5-9). For example, in Gal. 5.19-23 he offers two lists: 'the works of the flesh' and 'the fruit of the Spirit' to illustrate the tension between the flesh and the Spirit.

Gordon Fee divides the fifteen 'works of the flesh' into four categories. Three are illicit sex (sexual immorality, impurity, licentiousness), two are illicit worship (idolatry, sorcery), eight are breakdown in relationships (hostilities, strife, jealously, outburst of rage, selfish ambitions, dissensions, fractions, envies) and two are excesses (drunken orgies, revelries).[45] Significantly, eight of the items describe actions that lead to the breakdown of social relations – and these are problems that provoke accusations of witchcraft and demonisation. Three vices fall within illicit sex, two come under false worship, and two are classified as excesses. Traditionally, we view most of these vices as demonic. The fact that Paul does not is significant for us.

Christians are often warned against 'the works of the flesh' because they are expressions of human nature and worldliness. Such vices, according to Paul, may become the foothold of Satan and bring the wrath of God (Rom.1.18-32; Eph. 4.19-23; Col. 3.6). Paul's consistent warnings not to yield to the flesh mean that every Christian chooses whether to follow the flesh or obey the Spirit.

The implication of this for Christians is that most of the issues which are considered to be supernatural acts of witchcraft, ancestral curses, or demons may be appropriately considered as works of the flesh. For instance, an inner propensity to continue in an act that is against one's intent, like sexual immorality, may not necessarily be

---

[45] Gordon Fee, *God's Empowering Presence: The Holy Spirit in the Letters of Paul* (Peabody, MA: Paternoster, 1994), p. 441

the result of demonic influence. Similarly a person who has an anger problem, often tells lies, is prone to negligence may not be encountering demonic problems, but only be yielding to the flesh or exhibiting a weakness in temperament. Consequently, these acts may not need deliverance or exorcism, but rather need to be overcome by walking in the Spirit.

This is not to deny the possibility of physical attacks by the devil. Rather it is to emphasise that demonic attacks are first and foremost 'spiritual', or temptations, to live in ways which are contrary to the Word of God.

Physical Attacks

Clearly the Bible indicates that the devil instigates persecutions against Christians which result in suffering, and in some cases the death of believers (e.g. 1 Pet. 5.8-9; Rev. 2.9, 13; 3.9; 13.7). Again, the Bible reveals that the devil induces spiritual attack which may manifest in physical infirmity as in the case of the woman who was bent over (Lk. 13.11-16), or in the case of Paul's 'thorn in the flesh' (2 Cor. 12.7). That Paul prayed to God three times and was not 'delivered' means the issue was not between Paul and the devil, but rather between Paul and his God. This indicates that the eschatological tension displayed in the New Testament means Christians are still exposed to demonic powers which, although defeated, may attack under the permission of God.

8

STRONGHOLD 3: POSTMODERNISM AND THE SEXUAL REVOLUTION

Postmodernism is a false worldview that has gripped the West but is also impacting the African world. At its core is the belief that everyone should be able to live the way that he or she wants to live; no one religion or worldview can claim to be the only right way.

The postmodern philosophy asks, 'Who are we to say that this particular belief, order, or system is right?' Postmodernism, therefore, is an attack on modernists and Christians' claims about the existence of truth and value. Postmodernism says that nobody can claim to know the truth. It alleges that because we are limited in knowledge, space, and language, no one can confidently say that his or her way is right for all times, situations, and places. Truth therefore is relative; this is to say that truth is dependent on circumstances. Put another way, truth is situational; the situation that a person is in will inform him or her about what to do. This is to say that what is truth to you may not be truth to another. It depends upon where you are coming from and what you want to say.[46]

Because of postmodernism, we have pluralism of beliefs, which means there are many beliefs in the world which must be accommodated or tolerated. If somebody believes that his idol is the Supreme God, the person must be accommodated. If somebody says that if you beat drums today my deity will be disturbed, the person must be accommodated. If somebody says the best way of worship

---

[46] J. Richard Middleton and Brian J. Walsh, *Truth is Stranger Than It Used to Be: Biblical Faith in a Postmodern Age* (London: SPCK, 1997), pp. 28-45.

is to bow down, the person must be tolerated. Nobody can put his/her hands on the truth. Therefore, if for example, there is a problem, you can pray to your God and I can also pray to my God. No matter one's belief and practices, we must live together in peace and accept one another.[47]

The focus is on individual existence, subjectivity, and choice. Individuals must be allowed to do and practice what they feel is right for them. In making choices in life, people determine their individual selves, and human beings have enormous freedom. Thus, if people want to pursue pleasure they can do so. If they want to follow after fashion they can do so. If they want to expose part of their bodies, they can do so, so far as it is good for them. If you look at them and lust after them, it is your problem but not theirs.

This is a modern stronghold that the devil is using. Granted, some elements of postmodernism are acceptable from a Christian viewpoint. For example, we must not condemn people outright but instead accept them as they are. We can then use their interests as a point of contact to reach them with the gospel. Ultimately, however, postmodernism has placed the world on dangerous ground because if everything is true, nothing is true.

Do you think that someone who is convinced that all lifestyles are fine will immediately accept Christianity, which says that Jesus is 'the way, the truth, and the life, and no man comes to the Father' except through Him? Don't be too confident of fast success. People are not quick to abandon one set of beliefs for another. Postmodernism is a stronghold, and people hold on to it strongly.

Postmodernism, Technology, Money, the Media, and the Sexual Revolution

A cardinal tenet of postmodernism is that sex is not sacred; people should be free to express their sexual desires in whichever way pleases them. This has often been called the 'sexual revolution'. The media and modern technology – television, internet, DVDs, videos, mobile telephones, the press – have been the major vehicles for the promotion of the sexual revolution. The image-driven, sexual

---

[47] Philip Sampson, 'The Rise of Postmodernity', in Philip Sampson, Vinay Samuel & Chris Sugden (eds.), *Faith and Modernity* (Oxford: Regum, 1994), pp. 41-42.

presentations of television are more captivating than written and spoken words. We now have a culture that is rooted in edited, artificial, entertaining images. Sexy television personalities have become the mentors of our youth.

The internet is now by far the easiest way to get information. Through it, people can learn, chat, upload images, and download images. Almost everybody has access to this technological marvel.

The mobile telephone has made communication very easy. People can speak to one another no matter where they are.

Unfortunately, television, the internet, and the mobile telephone (with its free access periods) have facilitated the spread of inappropriate music, prostitution, pornography, and sexual immorality.

The sexual reformation was initiated by biologist Alfred Kinsey, a professor at Indiana University in the USA. In 1938, when Kinsey was asked to coordinate a course on marriage, his lecture on the biological aspect of married life became very popular with students. As Kinsey was convinced that sex research was an important and long-neglected field of study, he began to collect research data through sexual history interviews. The debatable results of Kinsey's research changed people's sexual behaviour forever. Kinsey shocked Americans by claiming that fifty percent of American married men, and a significant number of married women, had engaged in extramarital relationships; that thirty-seven percent of men had engaged in at least some homosexual experience; that ten percent of men were exclusively homosexual; and that premarital sex was common.[48]

Kinsey was accused of having sexual affairs with his workers, encouraging homosexuality, and teaching that it was natural. He was also accused of allowing his workers to have sex with his wife and encouraging his daughters toward promiscuity. This quote from the article 'Porn Star' says it all.

> No one felt the force of [Kinsey's] unyielding demands more strongly than Clara [Kinsey's wife, who] went along with the filming ... as befitted the wife of the high priest of sexual liberation. Clara was filmed ... having sex with Pomeroy [one of the

---

[48] The Kinsey Institute, 'Data from Alfred Kinsey's Studies', available at: www.kinseyinstitute.org/research/ak-data.html#Findings. Accessed: November 17, 2007.

workers] … [o]ne of the staff's wives refused to have sex with Kinsey … complaining of 'the sickening pressure' she was under to have sex on film with her spouse and other staff members. She told an interviewer, 'I felt like my husband's career at the Institute depended on it'.[49]

Yet, Alfred became a hero. The institute where he started his research was renamed 'The Kinsey Institute'. His two-volume work, *Sexual Behavior in the Human Male* and *Sexual Behavior in the Human Female* became the standard for studying human sexual behaviour. What else is left out? Kinsey set the agenda that caused a worldwide sexual revolution.

In the contemporary world, sex has been reduced to an ordinary act. People are encouraged not to attach any stigma on any type of sexual activity. Christians are told not to make people feel guilty for having sex. People therefore have all sorts of pleasure without a guilty conscience. Even if they have a guilty conscience, they will be encouraged to put it aside and continue to enjoy. All sorts of sexual acts are encouraged. These include homosexuality/lesbianism, bestiality, masochism (sadism), rape/de-filement, paedophilia (sex with children), exhibitionism, prostitution, ritual prostitution, incest, adultery, pornography, sexual self-gratification, fornication, cyber sex, and telephone sex.[50]

Sex is used for selling everything, from music to cars. Most of the adverts on television revolve around sex, and sexual songs are the ones that sell the most. This is exemplified in Madonna Louise Veronica Ciccone Ritchie, an American who is popularly known by her first name Madonna but is often referred to as the 'Queen of Pop'. She is not just a pop singer-songwriter, but a record and film producer, dancer, actress, author, and fashion icon. Guinness World Records listed Madonna as the most successful female recording artist of all time. A website that tracks her music sales says that she has sold more than 175 million albums, and 85 million singles.[51]

Regarding her permissive view of sexuality, Madonna said, 'Be strong, believe in freedom and in God, love yourself, understand

[49] Judith Reisman, 'Kinsey: Porn Star'. Available at: www.worldnetdaily.com/news/article.asp?ARTICLE_ID=29434. Accessed 6 August 2007.
[50] Nancy Friday, *Women on Top: How Real Life has Changed Women's Sexual Fantasies* (London: Arrow Books, 2003).
[51] 'Madonna's Chart Sales', available at: http//:absolutemadonna.com/charts/

your sexuality … don't judge people by their … sexual habits, love life and your family'.[52] People thought by becoming a mother Madonna would change. But she clearly articulated:

> Obviously, my tastes and my priorities have changed. Just because I'm a mother doesn't mean I'm not still a rebel and that I don't want to go in the face of convention and challenge the system. I never wanted to think in a robotic way, and I don't want my children to think that way, either. I think parents should be constantly questioning society.[53]

Madonna's rebellion is aimed at Christianity. One of the icons that she often wears is the crucifix because it arouses her sexually, 'Crucifixes are sexy because there's a naked man on them.'[54]

Madonna has many followers across the globe. In Ghana, Mzbel promotes Madonna's interests, and dresses and sings in a similar style. Though she has received much criticism, that has only made her more popular. She suffered a brutal attack in September 2006, and in an internet discussion room, 'soccerman' blamed the attack on traditional-minded Ghanaians:

> do you know what this woman had to go through? … many people were just hating cos she is a female rapper … and traditional thinking some ghanaians are, they werent used the whole female rap thing … and stupid ghanaian boyz taking advante of her … anywayz the story is just long![55]

Mzbel's albums sell quickly. This shows that despite the criticism, people are interested in her type of music.

Homosexuality as a preferred lifestyle continues to grow not only in many Western Nations but also in various places across Africa. Even in many churches there is a conflict over whether such a lifestyle is an acceptable practice. However, for those believers for whom homosexuality is deemed to be compatible with Biblical

---

[52] 'Madonna Ciccone', Available at: http://en.wikiquote.org/wiki/Madonna_Ciccone. Accessed November 17, 2007.

[53] 'Madonna Ciccone'.

[54] 'Madonna Ciccone'.

[55] 'Mzbell [sic] in New York', posted: Fri, August 31, 2007. Available at www.discussions.Ghanaweb.com/viewtopic.php?t=62065&highlight=woman. Accessed September 10, 2007.

teaching, such practice is another example of the kinds of strong-holds here described.

Bestiality and internet pornography are no longer confined to the West but are now worldwide problems.

The *Ghanaian Observer* reported on January 22, 2007, that sex trafficking was the world's third largest money-making crime be-hind the illegal trafficking of weapons and drugs. The article said that more people are trafficked globally today than at the height of the Transatlantic slave trade and that women who are forced into prostitution in London have sex with more than twenty men each day. The *Ghanaian Observer* was responding to an investigation conducted by the UK newspaper, *The People,* which stated that girls as young as fourteen were on sale in Africa for shipment to Britain, to be used as sex slaves at a cost of just £3,000.

In that report, a woman named Gladys Ofosu, a ringleader of sex trafficking, agreed to sell Linda Asamoah for £3,000 to Jim White, an investigator who posed as a businessman. This was a business deal in which Mr White was to take ownership of Ms Asamoah for two years. Ms Asamoah would work for Mr White and provide sexual services to paying customers. In return, she would receive a share of the money. If the deal worked, Mrs Ofosu would sell other girls to Mr White. The girls would be between fourteen and nineteen years old. Mrs Gladys Ofosu was eventually arrested.

Many people will do whatever they can to get money, and selling sex is one means of obtaining it. Girls will sell themselves and sometimes relatives will sell relatives. This is how the devil has built a stronghold of money through sex. No matter what one does, money is all that matters. This is the postmodern world in which we live.

Breakdown of Family Life

One of the greatest negative effects of the sexual revolution is the breakdown of traditional family life. The changes in cultural values have resulted in greater acceptance of divorce, out-of-wedlock births, single-parent homes. Glen Miles and Paul Stevenson rightly analyse this situation:

The emphasis is on the needs of the individual rather than the group. As a result, even the marriage commitment is seen as tenuous. If one or other of the partners feels their needs are not being fulfilled, he or she feels free to end the partnership. Marriage no longer guarantees security for the couple or the children. This increasing emphasis on individuals' rights is exemplified by the UN Charter for Human Rights. Yet it is essentially a Western philosophy and sits uneasily with attitudes in many non-western continents such as China, where the community often takes precedence over the individual. In developed countries, many of the economic, political and social functions once undertaken by the family have now been assumed by the State, banks, and schools ... The public and private worlds have become more separated, and the social and economic ties which once bound families together correspondingly weakened. The home, previously seen as the private retreat from a hostile public world, is sometimes now seen as not even that.[56]

This has seriously affected developing nations because these nations are not economically sound enough to meet the needs which hitherto had been met by strong families. In societies with broken families and cash-strapped governments, vulnerable, young, and needy people fall prey to the glitz and glamour on television.

Parents, churches, and teachers have a difficult time competing. Madonna says it all, 'I have the same goal I've had ever since I was a girl. I want to rule the world.'[57] Now she feels she has achieved that through her music. 'Now that I got everyone's attention, what do I have to say?' She voices out what she wants people to do, 'I don't care anymore if people dress like me, now I want them to think like me.'[58]

The media with its music and stars have an extremely powerful influence. Even responsible parents don't find it easy. Examine what Madonna says about her father, 'My father was very strong. I don't agree with a lot of the ways he brought me up. I don't agree with a lot of his values, but he did have a lot of integrity, and if he

---

[56] Glen Miles and Paul Stevenson, Children at Risk Guidelines, Vol. 1, Fiona Anderson, ed. Available at: http://tilztearfund.org/webdocs/Tilz/Topics/Family ENG_full%20doc.pdf. Accessed: November 19, 2007.

[57] 'Madonna Ciccone'.

[58] 'Madonna Ciccone'.

told us not to do something, he didn't do it either.'[59] Here, you realise that Madonna confesses that her father was a man of integrity. Yet she did not agree with most of the values he attempted to implant in her. From where was she taking her instructions? From the postmodern world around her.

Alfred Kinsey, who ignited the sexual revolution, had religious parents.

> Both of Kinsey's parents were extremely conservative Christians. This left a powerful imprint on Kinsey for the rest of his life. His father was known as one of the most devout members of the local Methodist church, and, as a result most of Kinsey's social interactions were with other members of the church, often merely as a silent observer while his parents discussed religion with other similarly devout adults. Kinsey's father imposed strict rules on the household including mandating Sunday as a day of prayer (and nothing else), outlawing social relationships with girls, and prohibiting knowledge of anything remotely sexual ... Such a strict upbringing was not entirely uncommon at the time. As a child, Kinsey was forbidden to learn anything about the subject that was to later bring him such fame. Kinsey ultimately disavowed the Methodist religion of his parents and became an atheist.[60]

Kinsey's Methodist parents tried to inculcate their faith into him, but he rejected it. Will your children reject yours? The internet, television, radio, DVDs – these can all be used quite positively, and we thank God for their development. But they are also being used to promote the false values of postmodernism – specifically that all ways are acceptable and no one way is right – not even Jesus.

---

[59] 'Madonna Ciccone'.
[60] 'Alfred Kinsey'. Available at: http://en.wikipedia.org/wiki/alfred_kinsey. Accessed: September 10, 2007.

9

STRONGHOLD 4: THE NEW AGE MOVEMENT

The New Age Movement is another false teaching that is exerting massive influence today.

One of the greatest challenges that Christians face is the New Age Movement. The New Age Movement is both a religious and a social movement. It professes a broad-minded openness to all religions and encompasses a wide array of notions: spiritualism, astrology, Christ-consciousness, Native American Spirituality, Eastern religious experiences, out-of-body/near-death experiences, reincarnation, and the occult disciplines. It also includes unorthodox psychotherapeutic techniques and pseudoscientific applications of the 'healing powers' of crystals and pyramids. It has various combinations of Gnosticism and Occultism.[61] Although it appears to be open-minded toward all religions, a careful examination of its basic underlying philosophy represents a calculated undermining of Judaism, Christianity and Islam.

The origin of the movement dates back to 1875 when Helena Petrovna Blavatsky transplanted Hinduism to the United States through the Theosophical Society, which she founded. A second notable figure was Blavatsky's co-worker, Alice Bailey, who wrote more than twenty books, allegedly through a spirit-guide.[62]

In 1922, Alice Ann Bailey founded the 'Lucifer Publishing Company' (now called the Lucis Publishing Company) which printed

---

[61] Gnosticism asserts that the physical world is evil and that salvation comes through possession of secret knowledge.

[62] Walter Martin, *The New Age Cult* (Minneapolis: Bethany House Publishers: 1989), p. 16.

and distributed her teachings, which speak extensively of Christ's return and the coming new world order. Those are biblical themes, but her teachings were distortions of biblical truth. Bailey wrote that prior to Christ's return, certain wise men will arise. 'The first step toward this longed-for consummation is the appearance of the Masters on the physical plane and then, somewhat later, the appearance of Christ.'[63] She continues that when Christ comes, he will come for all. 'The Christ works for all men irrespective of their faith; he does not belong to the Christian world any more than to the Buddhist, the Mohammedan or any other faith. There is no need for any man to join the Christian Church in order to be affiliated with Christ. The requirements are to love your fellowmen, lead a disciplined life, recognise the divinity in all faiths and all beings, and rule your daily life with Love.'[64] Again Bailey assured her followers that hell was a distorted teaching. She wrote:

> There is, as you well know, no angry God, no hell, and no vicarious atonement. There is only a great principle of love animating the entire universe; there is the Presence of the Christ, indicating to humanity the fact of the soul and that we are saved by the livingness of that soul, and the only hell is the earth itself, where we learn to work out our own salvation, actuated by the principle of love and light, and incited thereto by the example of the Christ and the inner urge of our own souls. This teaching about hell is a remainder of the sadistic turn which was given to the thinking of the Christian Church in the Middle Ages and to the erroneous teaching to be found in the Old Testament about Jehovah, the tribal God of the Jews. Jehovah is not God, the planetary Logos, the Eternal Heart of Love Whom Christ revealed.'[65]

Thus, Bailey's teaching was very appealing to people. There was no angry God who would punish people for their wrong doing. Consequently there was no hell. Her teaching was strategized to have influence on people.

---

[63] Alice Bailey, *The Externalisation of the Hierarchy* (New York: Lucis Publishing Company, 1957), p. 667.

[64] Bailey, *The Externalisation of the Hierarchy,* p. 558.

[65] Alice Bailey, *A Treatise on the Seven Rays,* Vol. IV, 'Esoteric Healings' (New York: Lucis Publishing Company, 1953), p. 393.

The Beliefs and Practices of the Present New Age Movement

Though Bailey was a key figure in the New Age Movement, she is not the single source of its beliefs and practices. The New Age Movement has no official leader, headquarters, or membership list.

Douglas R. Groothuis, identifies six distinct emphases of the New Age Movement:

• all is one
• all is God
• humanity is God
• a change in consciousness
• all religions are one
• cosmic evolutionary optimism.[66]

When New Agers say that 'all is one', they are saying that 'all of reality may be reduced to a single, unifying principle partaking of the same essence and reality'.[67] 'The diversity we perceive is actually unreal.'[68]

'All is one' is the New Age Movement's central theme and is found in the ancient *Gospel of Thomas*: 'Jesus said, 'I am the light that is over all things. I am All: from me all came forth and to me all attained. Split a piece of wood; I am there. Lift up the stone, and you will find me there' (77).[69]

This 'all is one' idea is also called 'monism'. The idea that God is the unifying principle who binds everything together is called 'pantheism'. But the God of the New Age Movement is not the personal God of Christianity; he is more like an impersonal energy force.[70]

This premise permeates the movement in all its various manifestations. It runs through it holistic health to the new physics, from politics to transpersonal psychology, from Eastern religions to the

[66] Douglas R. Groothuis, *Unmasking the New Age* (Downers Grove: InterVarsity Press, 1986), pp. 18-29.
[67] Marilyn Ferguson, *The Aquarian Conspiracy* (Los Angeles: J.B. Tarcher, 1980), p. 382, quoted in Walter Martin, *Kingdom of the Cults* (Minneapolis: Bethany House Publishers, 1997), p. 336.
[68] Martin, *Kingdom of the Cults*, p. 336.
[69] 'Gospel of Thomas', *Complete Gospels: Annotated Scholars Version* (Polebridge Press, 1994). Also available at: www.misericordia.edu/users/davies/thomas/Trans.htm. Accessed: November 20, 2007.
[70] Martin, *New Age Cult*, p. 25.

occult. 'All is interrelated, independent and interpenetrating.'[71] By implication it means that there is no difference between the creator and his creation, or God and humanity. It denies any separation between humanity and nature. It shows no line between a tree and a mountain; neither does it see any difference between Kofi (male) and Amma (female) nor John and a tree. All perceived differences between separate entities are only apparent and not real. They are all considered to be part of a continuous reality that has no boundaries.

Norman L. Geisler and David K. Clark detail fourteen primary doctrines of New Age religions, and they overlap a bit with the list of Groothuis:

- an impersonal god (force)
- an eternal universe
- an illusory nature of matter
- a cyclical nature of life
- the necessity of reincarnations
- the evolution of man into godhood
- continuing revelations from beings beyond the world
- the identity of man with god
- the need for meditation (or other consciousness-changing techniques)
- occult practices
- vegetarianism and holistic health
- pacifism (or anti-war activities)
- one world (global) order
- unity of all religions.[72]

These doctrines are all variations and corollaries of the premise that 'all is one'. All religion, occult practices, and belief systems are considered as one. All religions teach the same thing in different forms. The external teachings of religion may differ, but the essence is the same. Consequently, the exclusiveness of Christianity, Judaism, and Islam must be denied. Jesus of Nazareth, from the per-

---

[71] Groothuis, *Unmasking the New Age*, p. 18.
[72] David K. Clark and Norman L. Geisler, *Apologetics in the New Age: A Christian Critique of Pantheism* (Grand Rapids: Baker, 1990).

spective of the New Age Movement, must be considered as one of the many manifestations of God throughout the centuries.[73]

Many New Agers attach great importance to artifacts, relics, and crystals, the rainbow, pyramids, Tibetan bells, rays of light, exotic herbal teas, and coloured candles for chromotherapy. New Age practices re-birthing, inner healing, biofeedback, yoga, out-of-body experience, reflexology, black and white magic, fire-walking, trance-channelling, therapeutic touch, transpersonal psychology, witch-craft, parapsychology, and contact with extra-terrestrials. For example, one of the New Age movement apostles, Shirley MacLaine, claims she was inspired by an extra-terrestrial, named 'the Mayan', to write her book, *Out on a Limb*.[74]

Expectation of a Person after the Image of Messiah

As we saw in Bailey's writings, she was preoccupied with the return of a one-world leader whom she called 'The Christ'. The Christ is not the Christ of the Bible, but an advanced member of a spiritual hierarchy whose reappearance must be summoned by 'The Great Innovation'. The Great Innovation is a prayer, which in some circles functions as the New Age counterpart of the Lord's Prayer in the Bible. According to Newport, Bailey expected the New Age to dawn during a global crisis which could be rectified only by the 'Christ'. He will be a world-class teacher who will bring peace and solutions to the world's problems. Thus today, followers of Bailey speak about the inevitable advent of a great New Age Teacher – 'the Christ' or 'the Maitreya'. The term 'Maitreya' comes from the Buddhist tradition and refers to a Buddha of the future. The Maitreya is what the Hindus used to call the 'avatar' or the incarnate divinity for our age.[75]

In 1982, the Tara Foundation ran full-page advertisements in many newspapers announcing the soon appearance of the 'Christ'.[76]

---

[73] Christians, however, must recognise this as a direct contradiction of the Bible's revelation that Jesus Christ is the true manifestation of God in flesh (Jn 1.1-14).

[74] Groothuis, *Unmasking the New Age*, p. 24.

[75] John Newport, *The New Age Movement and the Biblical Worldview: Conflict and Dialogue* (Grand Rapids: Eerdmans Publishing Company), p. 511.

[76] Some New Age advocates believe that the second coming of Christ occurred in 1977 in the person of Maitreya.

To date, their Maitraya has not yet emerged as a celebrated leader, and he won't. But the aspirations of the New Age Movement are clearly seen. They are seeking a person, whether godly or devilish, who will be their messiah to save the planet.

In sum, the New Age Movement is extremely large and comprises an extensive network of mystic, occult figures devoted to the goals of a one global government and one global religion.

What can the Christian do? Remember, this is a stronghold, and people who follow the New Age Movement have wrapped their lives in its teachings. We need God's strength to pull them out and to keep ourselves from being pulled in. Walter Martin brings a suggestion: 'Prepare yourself for spiritual combat, study and show yourself approved by God, a workman who won't need to blush with embarrassment, rightly interpreting the word of truth. And above all, lift the shield of faith declaring, "Jesus Christ is Lord to the glory of God the Father".'[77]

---

[77] Walter Martin, *The New Age Cult* (Minneapolis: Bethany House Publishers, 1989), p. 108.

10

STRONGHOLD 5: OCCULTISM

The fifth stronghold we will look at is occultism, which is a false religious practice, and is related to the New Age Movement. The term 'occult' means something that is hidden from view, something not revealed or mysterious. Occultism has come to mean the practices or influences of supernatural powers. People often call it Satanism because it is believed that Satan controls such practices.

Occultism can be classified into four kinds. The first type is divination, the second spiritism, the third is sorcery, and the fourth is witchcraft and astral projection. These will be treated in order.

Divination

Divination is the attempt to foresee or foretell future events, or discover hidden knowledge by manipulation of objects or the interpretation of omens with the help of a supernatural power.[78] Divination can be divided into four groups.

The first types are astrology, enchanting, horoscopes, and zodiacs – and all can be termed as astrology. This is the attempt to discover the future through the stars in order to guide people's personal, social, and business lives. The Zodiac is the band of twelve constellations along the plane of the ecliptic through which the sun, moon, and planets pass across the sky. Each constellation is be-

---

[78] The Bible has numerous references to divination (e.g. Gen. 44.5; Deut. 18.10; 1 Sam. 6.2; Isa. 44.25; Jer. 27.9; 29.8; Ezek. 13.9, 23; 21.29; 22.28; Mic. 3.11; Zech. 10.2).

lieved to have symbolic significance that affect various aspects of life on earth. Every celestial movement and phenomenon, such as the rising and setting of the sun, moon phases, eclipses, and meteors, are said to have meaning or predict the future. These cosmic movements are noted regularly and detailed charts and tables are made. From these, human affairs and worldwide events are predicted.

A second practice of divination is reading tarot cards, crystal balls, palms, a rod and pendulum, and snail shells in order to peer into the future. The most popular one is palm reading. Practitioners look at the dominant hand and divide it into lines such as life line, heart line, success line, health line and the mounts. The mounts are named after the planets including Jupiter, Saturn, and Mercury; these are said to reveal the quality of leadership, reservedness, artistic competence, and persuasiveness. The life line is said to indicate major events, the head line reveals mental capabilities, and the heart line illustrates events connected with the emotional qualities of the individual.

The tarot card is also very popular. The term tarot comes from *taro-rota*, meaning 'the will of the law, and the law of the will'.[79] Tarot cards are the set of cards which consist of minor arcane and major arcane with twenty-two cards, a card numbered 0, and the fool.[80] They are said to be a symbolic representation of reality or to reveal the secrets of people and the universe. By reading them, one's subconscious powers are considered to be awakened. When this happens, it is thought that the inner forces of fate can be controlled. The colour, shape and symbolic forms on the cards are to be studied intuitively.[81]

The third groupings of divination are numerology and dreams. This group tries to study the significance of numbers to interpret dreams and predict the future. For example, the circle is a symbol of 'all things' or 'whole', because it can be imagined as a line drawn round everything. However, at the same time, the circle is a symbol of 'one thing' because it is a single figure. It is also considered as a

---

[79] Some historians claim that this 'game' came from Chaldea by way of Alexandria. Bob Larson, *Larson's Book of Spiritual Warfare* (Nashville: Thomas Nelson Publishers, 1999), p. 263.

[80] Others say that the deck has seventy-eight cards.

[81] Larson, *Larson's Book Spiritual Warfare*, pp. 264-65.

symbol of nought, 0; thus, it stands for emptiness, non-existence, nothing. The number thirteen was thought among some early Christians as the number of sin because it goes beyond the twelve apostles. In European magical tradition, the number thirteen is the number of necromancy, of bringing the dead back to temporary life, for consultation. Again, in European witchcraft, the number of a coven is regarded as thirteen.[82]

The last category of divination is telepathy, clairvoyance, clairaudience and the psychometric. Telepathy is the claim to have awareness of the thought or mental state of another person through extra-sensory perception. Clairvoyance refers to information received through extrasensory perception, focusing mentally on an event or the claim to perceive objective facts of which no one has knowledge, without use of the known senses. Or, it is the ability to see mentally without using the eyes, beyond ordinary time and space limits; some people also call it the 'Second Sight'. Clairaudience is the ability to hear mentally without using the ears. Psychometry is the ability to know about an object or its owner through contact with, or proximity to, the object. Or, it can be knowing about the owner of an object by handling the object. Often all four aspects will be operating through a person. The four aspects are interrelated.

Spiritism or Spiritualism

The second aspect of occultism is what can be called 'Spiritism' or 'Spiritualism'. This is grounded in the belief that people can, by means of 'spiritualists', make contact with spirits, such as people who have died and learn from them.[83] Spiritism can be classified into two main forms.

The first category is necromancy, familiar spirits, mediums, séances, trumpet mediums (TM), ghosts, and phantoms. Necromancy is the attempt to communicate with the dead, to receive infor-

---

[82] Hans Holzer, *Encyclopedia of Witchcraft and Demonology: An Illustrated Encyclopedia of Witches, Demons, Sorcerers, and Their Present-Day Counterparts* (London: Cathay Books, 1974), pp. 238-39.

[83] Compare the title of a medium's accounts of his work. John Edward, *One Last Time: A Psychic Medium Speaks to those We Have Loved and Lost* (London: Piatkus, 1999).

mation and help from them. Mediums and necromancers claim that the veil between the afterworld and this world is a thin one. Therefore they can contact the deceased for information. They claim to act as messengers attuning their minds to the spirit world in order to pass on what the spirits want to say.

A séance is the gathering of people who are trying to communicate with deceased loved ones or famous historical figures through means of a medium. The trumpet medium is the psychic or the person who brings forth 'spirit voices' through a trumpet at séances. Contemporary mediums claim they are not dealing with occult, but only applying a spiritual law.[84] However, the Bible condemns those who try to consult the dead (Lev. 19.31; 20.6, 27; Deut. 18.11; 1 Sam. 28.3, 7-9; 2 Kgs 21.6; 23.24; 1 Chron. 10.13; 2 Chron. 33.6; Isa. 8.19; 19.31).

The second type of spiritism includes consultation with other spirits, the use of Ouija boards, automatic writing, and trance-speaking. Consulting other spirits is practised among some 'spiritual churches' across the globe. In West Africa the practice is called 'calling of saints'. Here, sometimes a glass of water is placed on a table or an in drawn circle. Then, a sort of incantation prayer is said, while the spirit is invoked. It is claimed that saints like Moses, Elijah, Paul, Peter, and Mary can all be invoked.

A Ouija board is a piece of pressed cardboard with the numbers zero through nine, the letters of the alphabet, and words 'good', 'bye', 'yes', and 'no' printed on the surface. A small object with clear glass – called a 'counter' – is placed on top of the cardboard. Two players face each other with the board on their knees. Participants' fingers rest lightly on the counter, allowing it to move freely over the board. Questions are posed, and the counter eventually moves and stops over one of the letters or words, and the players see the letter or word through the glass. After that letter is seen, the counter moves on to the next letter until a sentence is spelled out and the question is answered.

Automatic writing is supposed to be an experience where a person in a trance is able to write down sentences, words, or letters, which are assumed to be messages from the spirits. Speaking in a

---

[84] Linda Williamson, *Contacting the Spirit World: How to Develop Your Psychic abilities and Stay in Touch with Loved Ones* (London: Piatkus, 1996), p. 21.

trance is the state where a person is brought by auto or hetero-hypnosis to speak into a situation or give revelation.

Spiritism is a very powerful stronghold that has gained grounds all over the world. Mediums are found in both the developed world and the underdeveloped world.

Sorcery and Magic

Another aspect of the occult is sorcery and magic, and it includes fetishism and voodoo.

Sorcery is sometimes used synonymously with the term magic. The term magic in this sense is different from stage magic, in which apparent magical effects are produced for entertainment through such means as sleight of hand. In such cases, magic is used by skilled people who use tricks and skills to entertain people.

Magic here is considered the art of learning techniques and ac-quiring knowledge in order to perform signs and wonders through appeals to supernatural powers. Techniques used in magic typically include chants, spells, gestures, and actions. These often have a symbolic relation to the final result. Also used are special substances that are believed to have a special relationship with the powers needed to accomplish the intended purpose.[85]

A distinction is often drawn between white and black magic. White magic is said to be employed for a good purpose, while black magic is used to harm others. Black magic is often related to sor-cery. However, sorcery also follows similar dual beliefs.

Sorcery includes the use of drugs, charms, and amulets, which are accompanied by incantations and appeals to supernatural pow-ers. There are allegedly two types: the good and the evil. The bad sorcerers use their powers to harm others, while good sorcerers use theirs to neutralise the activities of bad sorcerers and witches. Sor-cerers may use herbs, charms, amulets, or various concoctions, and they follow rituals to achieve their ends.[86]

---

[85] Biblical reference to magicians and magic (*chartôm*, *hartummîm*) include Gen. 41.8; Exod. 7.11, 22; 8.7, 18-19; 9.11; Dan. 1.20; 2.2, 27; 4.7, 9; 5.11.

[86] The Bible has numerous references to sorcery (*mekaššepîm*, *kâshaph*, Exod. 7.11; Isa. 47.9; Jer. 27.9; Dan. 2.2; Mal. 3.5. In Isa. 57.3 (AV) another term, *'ânan*, was translated sorceress.

Witchcraft and Astral Projection

The term witchcraft has been used in different ways in various historical and social contexts. Often it is in connection with magic or sorcery. Between the 13th and 14th centuries, opposition to alleged witchcraft hardened as a result of the growing belief that all magic and miracles came from Satan and were manifestations of evil. Those who practiced sorcery and magic were increasingly regarded as practitioners of witchcraft who were in league with Satan. At the dawn of the Renaissance (15th century to 16th century) some of these developments began to coalesce into the 'witch craze' that possessed Europe from about 1450 to 1700 CE. During the Age of Enlightenment, the persecution eventually declined and vanished as such beliefs were subjected to the skeptical eye.[87]

In the second half of the 20th century, a conscious revival of pre-Christian paganism occurred in the United States and Europe. The foundation of this revival was witchcraft, or *wicca*. *Wicca* is the early Anglo-Saxon word for witchcraft. The new *wicca* seeks to explore the nature and fertility religion of pre-Christian Europe. They claim this is different from Satanism or witchcraft, imagined by the persecutors of past centuries. Major *wiccan* themes include love of nature, equality of male and female, appreciation of the ceremonial, a sense of wonder and belief in magic, and appreciation of the symbolism and psychological realities behind the gods and goddesses of antiquity.[88]

In West Africa the witchcraft concept is different from the Western view. Witchcraft is the belief that some people may possess supernatural powers, which may be used either for good or evil. The witch is said to have the witch-spirit animal and witchcraft object. These become the spiritual equipment which, it is claimed, a witch operates with. Sometimes witches claim these things are material and other times they claim they are immaterial.

Witchcraft can be acquired in various ways, such as at birth, through transfer from a dying witch to a loved one, and by gifts. Witches are said to conduct their activities at local, district, regional,

---

[87] Gustav Henningsen & Bengt Ankarloo, eds. *Early Modern European Witchcraft: Centres and Peripheries* (Oxford: Clarendon Press, 1990), pp. 1-15.

[88] Robert S. Ellwood, 'Magic (sorcery)', *Microsoft® Encarta® 2006* [CD] (Redmond, WA: Microsoft Corporation, 2005).

national and international levels. However, the ways in which the self-claimed witches speak about their witchcraft is similar to astral projection in the West. They talk about their abilities to travel outside their bodies in order to bring about good or evil.

Astral projection is also known as out-of-body experience (OBE), and soul travel. Other people term this as psychic power. In this phenomena, the non-physical part of the body leaves the body, and in that spiritual state, it can consciously experience other physical realities.[89] A major goal of this experience is to lift and empower consciousness to generate new, positive interactions with the self. Through this experience people are expected to develop fully their potential and contribute to global well being.[90]

Witchdemonology

The term 'witchdemonology' is used to describe the occult beliefs and practices that have come to stay in Africa and other parts of the world. The term describes the beliefs and practices of 'deliverance ministries' in Africa, which is a synthesis of the practices and beliefs of African witchcraft and Western Christian demonology and exorcism.[91] Significantly all the occult practices which have been discussed above are termed as demonisation or witchcraft possession. The terms are used synonymously.

Maami Wata

Another concept which has developed in West Africa Christianity is the goddess of *Maami Wata*. *Maami Wata* is a concept of water spirit which originated from Nigeria. The myth says that God created human beings in groups and then allowed each individual to take an oath of life. After the oath of life, each group had to journey through water to the land of the living. Two different gates, guarded by two deities, one water deity and the other forest, respectively lead to the world. These deities have different interests and they try to win people to their sides. The vulnerable human beings, persuaded to commit themselves to any of the deities, owe an allegiance to

---

[89] Joe H. Slate, *Astral Projection and Psychic Empowerment: Techniques for Mastering the Out-of-Body Experience* (St Paul, MN: Llewellyn Publications, 1998), p. 1.

[90] Slate, *Astral Projection*, p. 3.

[91] Opoku Onyinah, 'Contemporary 'Witchdemonology' in Africa', *International Review of Missions*, 93.370/371 (Oct. 2004), pp. 330-45.

it. The water deity is called *Maami Wata*. *Maami Wata* is believed to be half human, half fish, mainly female and lives in the sea.[92]

Some Christians such as Emmanuel Eni and Victoria Eto picked this story and applied it to the demonisation of Christians.[93] Eto, for example, shows how she was involved with the goddess *Maami Wata* and with all sorts of sexual practices. She echoes the myth of the *Maami Wata* story. Eto elaborates on how after the fall of 'man' in Eden, the deity of *Maami Wata* was given the dominion over the sea, lakes, and rivers. She explains how to discover the manifestation and delights of the *Maami Wata* spirit, such as putting on beads or cowries as an ornament, and also how to exorcise this type of spirit.[94] The story of *Maami Wata* is very common among deliverance ministers in West Africa.

The Occult & Youth

In 1999, I interviewed a young man whose story shows how all types of occult practices have been adopted by people in order to sustain themselves in life. I put here much of the account of the interview for your perusal.

Question: I have been informed that you have a testimony to be told. What is it?

Answer   I, Bobby Essel, was born in *abosomfie* (a place where the gods are worshipped) at a town called Anomabu in the Central Region of Ghana.

              Whilst a child I started having encounters with spirit beings … At age five, I often played with their children using pebbles as their game objects. After this had continued for some time, I informed my grandmother with whom I stayed. My grandmother

---

[92] For reading on myth concerning *Maami Wata*, see C. Achebe, *The World of Ogbanje* (Enugu: Fourth Dimension, 1986), pp. 18-23; Misty Bastian, 'Married in the Water: Spirit Kin and Other Afflictions of Modernity in Southeastern Nigerian', *Journal of Religion in Africa* 27.2 (1997), pp. 123-24; Chinonyelu Moses Ugwu, *Healing in the Nigerian Church: A Pastoral-Psychological Exploration* (Bern: Peter Lang, 1998), pp. 162-63.

[93] Emmanuel Eni, *Delivered from the Powers of Darkness* (Ibadan: Scripture Union, 1988); See also Meyer, 'Delivered from the Powers of Darkness', pp. 237-55.

[94] Victoria Eto, *Exposition on Water Spirit* (Warri: Christian Shalom Mission, 1988).

explained that the spirit beings were my ancestral brothers who came to play with me. These spirit beings came to play with me under the groves of guava trees on our farm.

When I was a bit older, I no longer saw those 'brothers' to play with. Having missed their company, I asked my grandmother why? She explained that at that age, the spirits would no longer reveal themselves to me. However, they were still with me and would reveal themselves to me at an appropriate time. To prove that fact, the spirits did something spectacular.

One afternoon, when I went to fetch water from a stream, a big black pig dogged its steps until it entered my house. It was at that point that the pig stopped. Suddenly, my grandmother was possessed by the spirits and she said the pig had been sent by our spirit-being friends in order to confirm their long-lasting relationship, protection and companionship to me. That pig was their 'horse' used in their spiritual errands. (My grandma was a traditional priestess). The pig was killed and its pork shared and eaten.

With time I developed to a point where I became a kleptomaniac. I started joining a gang of thieves, who indulged in several social vices including flirtations with older girls. This newly adopted lifestyle baffled my grandmother, who resolved to send me elsewhere. So I was taken to another grandmother who was a *Nackaba*[95] prophetess at Abandze. She hoped I would change by that remedial action. But that was to be a fiasco. I became worse.

I used to sleep in the same bed with my grandmother. She put a bangle round my waist as though I were a girl. Those who saw that waist bangle, and

---

[95] *Nackaba* is one of the popular names of the Twelve Apostles Church.

taunted me, ended up being brought to the prophetess, my grandmother, within two days, sick.

In due course, I sensed I had covenanted with some spiritual forces. In a series of dreams, I saw that I had entered a different world where I met a man. The man told me that he would make me a great man. What he instructed me in dreams, I should do in the physical without divulging such secrets to anyone. Truly, I complied and was able to burgle so many people without being caught or arrested. Nobody could inflict any harm through 'juju' on me. That man I saw in my dreams had helped me to appease all the witches around that area.

The man empowered me to speak to spirits in the heart of the earth and in mountains. When I started being literate, it was then that I realised that my grandma, the prophetess, was dabbling in spirits. She had been speaking in the deep of the night, as though in prayer, to some spirits. She explained to me that those spirits were angels from the sea, who often came over to give her directions in her work.

With time when I had become too troublesome to control. I was sent to an uncle, who was a magistrate at that time, he said he would train me to be a master in my own right. My stay with him made things worse. I was introduced to the rudiments and practice of the lodge society.

Question: Did you feel you were a wizard before this time?
Answer: Yes, I had a meeting with witches once. But I didn't like what I saw, such as human flesh and blood, so I didn't attend it for the second time.

Witchcraft has different categories. There are those who are vampires and cannibals. There are others who operate by the spirit in them. They can inflict pain on people who offend them. This, they can do in the physical.

If somebody offended me I would think of something evil to happen to the offender. In no time, my concentrated evil thoughts would have the exact effect I thought about on him. If I want to flirt with any lady, I would think until I dreamt about having a sexual affair with her. If I propose even a day after such dreams, they would simply accept it.

Question: Could you concentrate without dreaming and yet influence a lady to flirt with?

Answer: Yes! In that case, the girl would come to me on her own accord. This happened when I joined the lodge. Prior to that era, I used to visit those girls in the spirit. In all those endeavours, the man I saw in my dreams, escorted and encouraged me along.

Question: You said you visited a witches' coven once. Was it before you joined the lodge?

Answer: It was during the time I stayed with my grandmother who was a traditional priestess.

Question: How did you go to that meeting?

Answer: All I realised was my grandmother was going with me. When we reached I knew the person whose body had been transformed into mutton. This explains why I was reluctant to partake of that 'meal' at the party.

So when I went to live with my lodge uncle, who was a magistrate at that time. He said he would train me to be a master in my own right. In the lodge society, I learnt that everybody is a master, but we have lost that power by our own making. Jesus was regarded the most Superior Master. In the event of any attack or challenge, we invoke his name for our defence. The name we used to represent Jesus was *Abremento*.

It was in the Lodge that I developed visualisation, concentration and imagination capabilities. Through these methods I could obtain admission into schools. That was through astral travels.

Question: How did you travel by astral means?

Answer: We had some incantations that we recited at a secluded place, where distractions and disturbances were absolutely absent. In due course, the soul would leave the body, for any imagined destination. The body was left behind.

There are different grades of masters. Whilst in an astral travel, if a subordinate master was attacked and overpowered by a superior, the former would end up a mad person in the physical realm. Some of the mental patients we find out at prayer camps have such things as the remote causes of their madness. For protection against these forces in the astral world, we had special rings. These rings were respected by all the forces.

Questions: How did you communicate with the people you visited through astral travels?

Answer: For admissions I called the souls of headmasters in whose schools I wanted admissions by candlelight. I must have seen their photographs to be able to recognise them. Then I would tell his image my wish. When I later went to see them in the physical realm, my admission was just a formality. He would admit me without a second thought.

I could collect money and other things by astral travels. I played this game on my biological father who was at the 37 Military Hospital. He had neglected me. And I resolved to beat him according to his game. By the time he was aware, he had given me several thousands of Cedis. I later wrote to tell him how I had influenced him to do my bidding.

It happened that whilst returning from a brother of mine at Tema, I met a young beautiful lady. See, in the spiritual realm, not all spirits are recognisable. Whilst some have secondary and tertiary 'eyes' others have even more ... When I wooed her, she gave in to my sexual advances. She gave me her address, but all effort at contacting her later proved futile.

Then I started having dreams about her. When she first revealed herself to me, so many girls she claimed were her maids accompanied her. As I could not easily recognise her, she referred to the sexual encounter I had with a certain girl, whilst I returned from Accra a couple of weeks back. It was then that I knew her real identity. She was *Maami Wata* (the Sea goddess). She said she was my covenant wife, from then on. She thus ordered me never to flirt with a woman twice. She would not have any rival. Even though she no longer visited me in human flesh, we enjoyed sex in the spirit in my dreams.

When I got converted, she continued to harass me to return the broken relationship. Just a couple of weeks ago, she wrote a physical letter to me. There were several promises of wealth she promised me if I restored the relationship. I even showed the letter to Prophet Kesse.

Question: Is the letter here?
Answer: Oh we tore it in shreds. That night she came and expressed her disappointment to me. I didn't want to be prosperous.

That's unfortunate. It could have served as evidence.

It is when I'm in desperate need of money that I am often harassed by these foul spirits through dreams and even my senses. In the letter she told me a certain number of steps to count, at the end of which I would bump into fat money (75,000 Cedis). But I would not obey. She threatened to kill me if I turned down that offer of hers ...

Question: So did the sea goddess come only in a dream?
Answer: I never met her physically again.

Question: Could she come only when you were asleep?
Answer: Yes, she would ask if I was still determined not to marry her again. I would retort by telling her, I had been married to Jesus. I could not be married to two Lords. The only means, by which I could dismiss her, was through quoting the word of God.

              Such forces attack me by thoughts. On some occasions, they send spirit beings in the form of girls. Experience helps me to identify such agents. They came as impostors or impersonators.

Question: How did you get converted?
Answer: I was once reading the New Testament when I reached Galatians 5.19-21. I felt guilty of all the charges listed there. As I thought about the words, the spirits quickly came to forewarn me of what they would do to me, if I abandoned them. It was in desperation that I left Abidjan for Ghana. That was how I ended up at the Agona Wassa Prayer Camp.

              Through prayers the spirits in me left my body at all angles, through my armpits, nostrils, all over. As they left me, I felt pricking and jabbing sensations in my body. At a point I saw in a trance a man who pulled out of me a heart, which had been suspended on what looked like a chain. I felt so light at that end. That's how I was delivered. I was encouraged to fill my mind with the word of God. From my previous experience with the lodge, I knew the evil forces feared confessions.[96]

---

[96] Interview with Bobby Essel, Agona Wasa, August 25th, 1999.

The story of Bobby gives us indications of many things. He was born into the family where the traditional gods were worshipped. It was thought that often the ancestors paid him visits. He claimed to have received witchcraft and visited a witches' coven. He got into bad company and led a bad life. He was initiated into a lodge and practiced spiritism and astral projection. He got married to *Maami Wata* and got involved in excessive sexual practices. This is witchdemonology, a combination of the beliefs and practices of both witchcraft and demonology. Witchdemonology is the common experience in many parts of the world.

The internet testifies that occultism is practiced through out the world. While some appear in the forms of churches, others come in the forms of occult magic, or psychic forms.

The places where they are usually caught up into occult practices are the schools and the universities. Most often, these young adults turn to the occult because of a deep sense of alienation from mainstream culture and spiritual emptiness within.

The Occult and Crime

The occult is often connected to crime, and murders are sometimes tied to Satanic activity. One such crime is ritual murder which is common in Africa. There was the belief that as people become more civilised ritual murder may decrease, but this has not been the case. Throughout sub-Sahara Africa, often there are reports of people who have been killed with some parts mutilated. Dr Kwasi Fobi of Ghana laments on this in his article on the internet, 'When will this Insanity End?' Dr Fobi was disturbed about the disappearance of women in various parts of Accra, Ghana, especially during power outages. According to him, although the police (initially) denied any evidence of ritual murder, a friend he spoke to confirmed that syringes were found near most of the corpses, which suggested that blood might have been drained after the killings. He reiterated that ritual murder was not typical to Ghana alone but recounted instances in Africa, where ritual murder has been suspected. He concluded, 'Our society has various social ills but there is none that I detest more than tribalism and these senseless ritual killings. Brothers and sisters, how much longer can we allow these killings to go on? WHEN WILL THIS INSANITY END?' [97]

In the UK, various reports posted on the internet indicate that ritual murders continue among the African communities. When children, such as Victoria Climbie and Adam died, some believed that they had been killed in a ritual murder. A confidential report for the Metropolitan Police suggested children were being trafficked into the UK from Africa and used for human sacrifices. The report talked of rituals and witchcraft being practised as big business. [98]

However, ritual murders in Europe are not limited to Africans only. Another example is that which was reported about a couple in Germany, who claim that they killed their friend on the orders of the devil. Daniel Ruda, 26, and his wife Manuela, 23, admitted killing Frank Haagen, 33, but said they were not responsible for his death.

His body was found decomposing in the couple's flat in Bochum, in the west of the country. He had been battered to death with a hammer and was covered with dozens of stab wounds. A scalpel protruded from his stomach, and a pentagram, the sign of the devil, was carved into his chest.

The couple went into hiding for a week after killing Mr Haagen, who had worked with Mr Ruda. They confessed to killing but not murder. 'I got the order to sacrifice a human for Satan', Daniel Ruda told the court in a statement. Manuela Ruda said, 'It was not murder. It was the execution of an order. Satan ordered us. It simply had to be. We wanted to make sure that the victim suffered well.'

Mrs Ruda told the court she became a Satanist in Britain. She described drinking blood from volunteers she met on the internet.

She said, 'I was in England and Scotland, met people and vampires in London. We went out at night, to cemeteries, in ruins and in the woods. I also slept on graves and even allowed myself to be buried in a grave to test the feeling ... I signed over my soul to Satan two and a half years ago.' [99]

---

[97] http://www.ghanaforum.com/cgi-bin/archive?read=2786. Accessed on 9 February 2007

[98] 'Boys Used for Human Sacrifice'. Available at: http://www.utexas.edu/conferences/africa/ads/787.html. Accessed on February 9, 2007.

[99] 'Judgement Day for German Satanists.' Available at: http://news.bbc.co.uk/1/hi/world/europe/1792416.stm. Accessed on February 9, 2007 on 9 February 2007.

Another example occurred in Chiavenna, Italy on June 6, 2000, when three teenage girls brutally murdered a nun, Sister Mary Laura Manetti, after they had formed their own satanic group, which, they said, was influenced by the lyrics of heavy metal musician Marilyn Manson.[100]

In the United States, a fairly recent example is what happened in Pearl, Mississippi. On October 1, 1997, Luke Woodham stabbed his mother to death, then went to school and opened fire with a rifle, killing two of his classmates and wounding seven. Luke was part of a Satanic cult called 'The Kroth'. Prior to joining, Luke was heart-broken. A friend who persuaded Luke to join promised him that he could 'do something great'.[101]

The devil is a deceiver; ritual murder is an ancient stronghold that has been revived by Satan.

Occultism in Government

Throughout the world occultism has reached into governments. There have been unsubstantiated reports about some Heads of States who have been practising occultism. But there is one prominent wife of a US president whose reports have been confirmed. One outstanding example was the revelation in *Time Magazine* that Nancy Reagan, when she was First Lady of the United States, consulted an astrologer, whose advice influenced many of President Reagan's movements.[102] This is an indication that occultism is being or has been practiced at all levels. It is a stronghold of the devil.

---

[100] http://www.petersvoice.com/nunmurder3.htm. Accessed on 12 February, 2007.

[101] 'Woodham testifies he was involved in Satanism.' Available at: http://www.cnn.com/US/9806/11/school.shooting.03/index.html#links. Accessed on February 12, 2007.

[102] Barrett Seaman, 'Good Heavens! An Astrologer Dictating the President's Schedule?' Time Magazine, May 16, 1988. Available at: http://www.time.com/time/magazine/article/0,9171,967389,00.html. Accessed: November 19, 2007.

11

STRONGHOLD 6: MURDER

The next stronghold we shall discuss is murder; paramount among them is serial killing. Murder involves a deliberate, premeditated design to cause the death of a person. This happens in the form of genocide, a ritual, revenge, contract, cover up of sin, or a pleasure. Genocide is the crime of destroying or conspiring to destroy a group of people, because of their ethnic, national, racial, or religious identity. Revenge is to inflict death on another in return for what the person has done. Contract killing is where one person pays money to somebody to kill another for him/her. Cover up is to kill another to keep secret the sins or offences that one has committed. A ritual murder is the killing of somebody for sorcery or magic.[103]

There has been an increase in various forms of murder in almost all the continents. Although on the surface some forms of murder may not appear satanic or occultic, underneath is the devil who has planted in the minds of people who can take the life of others without much worry. The thing which urges or lures them to kill others without showing sympathy is what I am calling a stronghold of the devil.

People thought murder might abate overtime, but it continues to grow in all the continents in the twenty-first century. There is often news on students who become frustrated in life, go to their schools and kill other students and teachers as well. The devil is continuously planting evil in the minds of people.

---

[103] Ritual murder has been treated in Chapter Ten.

It is difficult to understand the real motive of some murders which take place across the globe. Examples of these are the murders of Martin Luther King, Jr and Present John F. Kennedy of USA. There are other people who are not as famous as these people who are being murdered daily. Revenge, contract killing, or cover up may be some of the reasons. These are strongholds which must be identified and worked on.

One of the strongholds which I shall like to discuss is serial killing. Often such serial killers operate in some underdeveloped countries, but they are not easily arrested since most of the countries lack the right equipment to investigate. Within the developed countries, they are often found out. Thus the examples I cite are taken from USA, since they have been able to instigate to bring out valid reports.

In 1969, Charles Miles Manson and his 'family' of followers murdered nine victims. He started his church and assumed the role of both Satan and Christ. Most of his followers were hopelessly confused about their lives, adopting Manson as a combination of mentor, father-figure, lover, and Christ. Mason had rubbed shoulders with Robert De Grimston, the founder of the Church of Satan, the Process Church of Final Judgment, where Satan, Lucifer, and Jehovah were worshipped simultaneously. Mason grew obsessed with death. He and his followers kept on killing until they were found out. Some of the murders were reported to be ritualistic in nature, with 36 leather thongs wrapped around each victim's throat. Manson's favourite statement was this: 'look down on me, you will see a fool. Look up at me, you will see your lord. Look straight at me, you will see yourself.'[104]

Another alarming trait was the eating of human flesh by Albert Fish. He gloated of how he killed and ate people. In a letter to a couple he chronicled one of his gruesome murders and his cannibalistic consumption of the victim.[105]

Why should a human being boast of eating another human being? Was he normal? By eating human flesh it concludes that Mr Fish was abnormal. However, if you examine how he committed the crime in such a way as not to be found out, it appears that he

---

[104] File://E:\\Chareles%20Mason.htm. Accessed on 9 February 2007.
[105] File://E:\Albert%20Fish.htm, Accessed on 26 October, 2006.

was sensible enough to do it in a way not to be caught. What led to this and other similar crimes? I have realised there was something in common with these sorts of people. Most of them had a very bad upbringing and background. This will come out clearly as I cite the example of the next man.

Henry Lee Lucas' murder cases were extraordinary. Lucas was described as America's most controversial murderer. But read about his background. Henry Lee Lucas was born on August 23, 1936, at Blacksburg, Virginia, USA. The Lucas family home was a two-room, dirt-floor cabin in the woods outside of town. Henry's parents were alcoholic; they also brewed bootleg whiskey. His mother, Viola Lucas, was doing occasional turns as the neighbourhood prostitute, while his father Anderson Lucas, dubbed 'No Legs', dragged himself around the house and tried to drown his personal humiliation in a non-stop flow of liquor.

Viola, as the mistress of the house and the manager of the family, ran her family with a rod of iron. The Lucas family consisted of nine children, but several were farmed out to relatives, institutions, and foster homes over the years. Henry was one of those 'lucky' enough to remain with his parents, and mother Viola appears to have hated the child from the moment of birth, seizing every opportunity to make his life a living hell on earth.

Both Anderson (husband) and Henry (son) were the targets of Viola's violent outbursts, enduring wicked beatings, forced to witness the parade of strangers that were called upon to share Viola's bed. Sickened by one such episode, Anderson Lucas dragged himself outside to spend a night in the snow, there contracting pneumonia, which cost him his life.

Henry survived, after a fashion, but his mother's cruelty seemed to know no bounds. When Henry Lucas entered school, in 1943, she curled his stringy hair in ringlets, dressed him as a girl, and sent him off to class that way. Barefooted, until a kind teacher bought him shoes, Henry was beaten at home for accepting the gift.

If Henry found a pet, his mother killed it, and he came to understand that life, like sex, was cheap.

When Henry's eye was gashed, reportedly while playing with a knife, Viola let him suffer until doctors had surgically to remove the withered orb, replacing it with glass. On one occasion, after he was beaten with a piece of lumber, Henry lay semi-conscious for three days before Viola's live-in lover – 'Uncle Bernie' – took him to a local hospital for treatment.

Uncle Bernie then became a friend. He introduced the boy to sexual activity and how to kill and torture various animals. At age 15, anxious to try sex with a human being, Henry picked up a girl. When the girl resisted his inept advances, he strangled her and buried her corpse in the woods. The murder remained unsolved for thirty-two years, until Henry confessed it in 1983.

In June 1954, he got involved in a series of burglaries that earned him a six-year prison term. He walked away from a road gang on September 14, 1957, and authorities tracked him to his half-sister's home, three months later. A second escape attempt, in December 1957, saw Henry recaptured the same day, and he was discharged from prison on September 2, 1959.

Back in Tecumseh, where his mother was, Henry was furious when his 74-year-old mother turned up on the doorstep, nagging him incessantly with her demands that he should return to Blacksburg, his hometown. Both of them were drinking on the night of January 11, 1960, when she struck him with a broom and Henry struck back with a knife, leaving her dead on the floor. Arrested five days later, Henry confessed to the murder and boasted of abusing his mother's corpse, a detail he later retracted as 'something I made up'.

Convicted in March 1960, he drew a term of 20 to 40 years in prison. Two months later, he was transferred to Ionia state hospital for being criminally insane, where he remained until April 1966. Paroled on June 3, 1970, Henry went back to Tecumseh and moved in with relatives.

In 1971, he was booked on a charge of molesting two teenaged girls. The charge was reduced to simple kidnapping at his trial, and Henry went back to the state penitentiary at Jackson and was paroled in August 1975.

In late 1976, he met 29-year-old Ottis Toole at a Jacksonville, Florida soup kitchen. The homosexual Toole was an arsonist and serial killer in his own right, and they hit it off immediately, swapping ghastly tales of their adventures in killing. Over the next six and a half years, Henry and Toole were fast friends, occasional lovers and frequent travelling companions, taking their murderous act on the road.

Eventually, in 1982, he was arrested and jailed as an ex-convict, possessing a handgun. Four nights later, he summoned the jailer, pressing his face to the bars of his cage as he whispered, 'I've done some bad things.' Over the next 18 months, Henry confessed to a seemingly endless series of murders, bumping his estimated body-count from 75 to 100, then from 150 to 360, tossing in murders by friends and associates to reach a total 'way over 500'.

According to Henry's confessions, he launched a career of random murder, travelling and killing *as the spirit moved him*, claiming victims wherever he went. Otis Toole, then serving time in Florida on an arson charge, was implicated in many of the crimes, and Toole chimed in with more confessions of his own. Some of the crimes, said Henry, were committed *under orders from a nationwide Satanic cult, the 'Hand of Death'*, which he joined at Toole's request. Toole sometimes ate the flesh of victims they had killed, but Henry abstained.

Some of Henry's stories were termed as 'false' confessions and later he turned around his confessions. Authorities reacted in various ways to Henry's turn-around. The truth may never be revealed, but in the meantime, Henry's jailers are convinced of his involvement in at least 100 murders. The true number of murders he committed is still unknown.

On June 26, 1998, then governor of Texas, George W. Bush commuted his death sentence to life without the possibility of parole. One of Henry's statements was:

> Sex is one of my downfalls. I get sex any way I can get it. If I have to force somebody to do it, I do … I rape them. I've done that. I've killed animals to have sex with them … I've had sex with them while they're still alive …'[106]

He thinks sex is one of his downfalls. But is that all? Was it just sex? The background was evil and dark. He endured evil and suffering in childhood. Love was not a factor, even when he became a recipient of love he had to suffer for it. The devil's stronghold of evil had been built in him. Such a person becomes a good instrument of the devil – a stronghold. His eyes had been blinded by the

---

[106] Quoted in Peter Vronsky, *Serial Killers: The Method and Madness of Monsters* (New York: Penguin, 2004), p. 276.

god of this world. Many people who become serial killers have similar backgrounds, very bad upbringing.

This is a stronghold and dangerous one, of course, that needs the power of the gospel to breakdown.

12

STRONGHOLD 7: SATANIC CHURCHES AND ATHEISTIC PRACTISES

Satanic worship consists of individuals, organised groups or churches with diverse varieties of satanic beliefs. In various universities and other institutions the practice of Satanism is gaining greater attention. The advocates are individuals who have seriously committed themselves to the beliefs, tenets, rituals, and ideologies of satanic systems and practices. Although these people may not in reality believe in Satan or God, thus they may be atheists. Yet their blatant mockery and disobedience to God are signals that the devil has blinded their eyes and uses them as a stronghold (2 Cor. 4.3-4).

In the United States, for example, some satanic churches are recognised by the government as religious organisations, and consequently, are not only protected by the law but also receive tax-exemption status as churches do.[107] There are many satanic churches and a variety of other religious organisations that openly practice Satanism.

Owing to the sensitive nature of occultism, the Internet has become the prime source for the extensive growth of the satanic community. The World Wide Web provides a significant forum for recruiting new members, disseminating information, and exchanging ideas. There are hundreds of web sites for satanic organisations, churches, support groups, and occult supplies. In addition to individual web sites, there are libraries, chat rooms, message boards,

---

[107] The USA becomes important since many things which take place there have effort on other parts of the world.

and resource sites. The more active resource web sites include the Satanic Network,[108] the Australian Satanic Council,[109] Devil Spawn,[110] and the 600 Club.[111] There are so many satanic web sites that there are several awards given to the best sites, including Lucifer's Top List and Tomb of Darkness. Some of the hosts of the satanic awards have their own web sites listing the winners, with convenient hyperlinks. They include The Fire Within Top 100, The Best Satanic Sites on the Internet,[112] and Blacklist Top 100, which is indeed disturbing because it links to violent pornography, torture, and images of actual murders. People can even invite demons to take over their lives on the internet.[113] It appears as entertainment but the devil will respond if he is invited.

To the surprise of many Christians, there is Radio Free Satan, available 24 hours a day, advertised as the voice of Satan on the Internet.[114] In 2006, The Church of Satan announced the premiere of Satanism Today, another Internet radio station, whose stated goals are to publicise the philosophy of their church and its membership; they list the following topics: news from the satanic perspective, applications of satanic theory in daily life, and practical applications of greater and lesser magic, featuring a new guest each week and much more.[115]

Satanism is practiced throughout the world. The internet shows its relation in all the continents. While some appear in the form of churches, others come in the form of entertaining groups, occult magic, or psychic forms.

The Youth is often the target of satanic groups since most of the things they do fall within youth culture. A survey conducted in 1990 by Neil Anderson among Christian teenagers in the USA indicated that almost 50% (861 out of 1725 people) had involved themselves

---

[108] http://www.satannet.com/.

[109] http://www.satanic.org.au.

[110] http://www.geocities.com/satanism_au/index.html.

[111] http://the600club.net/cgi-bin/community/index.pl.

[112] http://members.hostedscripts.com/top.cgi?user=TheDevil.

[113] http://www.damnage.com/BlackList/index.shtml, Accessed on 12 February 2007.

[114] http://radiofreesatan.com.

[115] The two most established, best-known American Satanic churches are The Church of Satan (CoS) and The Temple of Set (ToS).

in what he calls 'occult activity'.[116] Youth subculture Satanists are sub-categorised as dabblers; they are teenagers and young adults who are usually introduced to Satanism via music, film, the internet, mobile phones, and other media. For example, many mobile phones give free unlimited calls at night; who apart from the youth may call at night? Married couples and responsible adults would be sleeping.[117] It is the period, when the youth instead of sleeping to have enough rest for the following day's studies and activities, will be having chats that can lead to all sorts of immoral behaviour on the phone. The places where they are usually caught up into occult practices are the schools and the universities. Most often, these young adults turn to the occult because of a deep sense of alienation from mainstream culture and spiritual emptiness within them. They are drawn into this by their peers. They either eventually return to more traditional beliefs or are recruited into one of the many satanic religious organisations or groups. Their rituals usually escalate depending upon the length of time they are involved in Satanism, beginning with simple magical incantations and sometimes evolving into animal and human sacrifice.

Common crimes of youth subculture Satanists include vandalism, arson, grave desecration, animal mutilation, school violence, rape, and sometimes murder. The type of crime will depend upon their level of seriousness at the time of their involvement.

In Ghana, one school girl arranged with her colleagues and beat to death her teacher who failed to give in to her wishes. This is violence in the strongest sense, although not directly linked with the devil, he is underneath to strengthen such act.

Numerous murders and suicides have been attributed to the media and cultural influence of Satanism.[118] This is a stronghold that the devil has built in many people, especially the youth.

---

[116] Neil Anderson, *The Bondage Breaker: Overcoming Negative Thoughts, Irrational Feelings and Habitual Sins* (London: Monarch Books, 1993, New Edition, 2000), p. 128.

[117] It must be pointed out, however, that many use mobile phones at night, such as shift workers, the sick, those with sleeping disorders, and unemployed who sleep late and therefore go to bed late.

[118] http://www.anthropoetics.ucla.edu/ap0702/skandalon.htm. on 12 February, 2007.

13

SUMMARY OF THE DEVIL'S STRONGHOLDS

The scheme that the devil uses is to build strongholds in people so that they will not know what God has done for humanity and accept it. The strongholds are false philosophies, beliefs, doctrines, teachings, and practices that cause arrogance and rebellion against the gospel of our Lord Jesus Christ. They are strongholds because they are rooted in people's minds and are not easily dislodged. Only the Gospel can expose their errors and enlighten and strengthen people to change. 'The truth will set you free' (Jn 8.32).

Examples of contemporary strongholds were discussed:

The first stronghold was false teachings in the Church. False teachings are those that stray from the Bible. Some false teachers began as genuine Christians but diverted along the way, while others were never genuine believers in the first place. Some false teachers come to the church to gain money through their human devices, and others are sometimes planted by Satan.

We discover if a teaching is true or false by comparing it with the Bible. Though God's biblical revelation has been progressive, his truth has never contradicted itself. False teachings often stress man-made rules, they neglect Christ's universal church, and claim to be an elite or a selected group. Jesus' test was presented as the final judgment: 'You can detect them by the way they act, just as you can identify a tree by its fruit' (Mt. 7.20).

The second stronghold was the flesh. Satan and his demons try to influence Christians to live contrary to the Word of God, and the Bible calls that 'walking according to the flesh'. Therefore, Christians need to walk according to the Spirit. Christians are warned against 'the works of the flesh', not because they are demonic, but because they are expressions of our human nature and the world around them.

The third stronghold was postmodernism. Postmodernity claims that truth is relative, dependent on circumstances. The effect is that all viewpoints must be accommodated. Individuals must be allowed to do and practice what they feel is good for them. The media and modern technology – television, internet, DVD, video, mobile telephone, the press – have been the major vehicles for the promotion of postmodern ideas, including the sexual revolution.

Sex has been reduced into any ordinary act, which people do merely to satisfy themselves, and the traditional family has broken down. The home (with husband, wife, and children), previously seen as the place of refuge from a hostile public world, has been weakened and in many cases lost. Many parents have lost control of their children, who have been captured by the lifestyles they see in the media.

The fourth stronghold was the New Age Movement, which is important because it is very influential. The movement is both a religious and a social movement. It professes a broad-minded openness to all religions. It encompasses a wide array of practices: spiritualism, astrology, Christ-consciousness, various traditional spiritualities, Eastern religious experiences, out-of-body/near-death experiences, reincarnation, and the occult disciplines.

Occultism was the fifth and final example of a demonic stronghold. We classified the occult into four kinds: divination, spiritism, sorcery, and magic – as well as witchcraft and astral projection.

Divination is the attempt to foresee the future, or discover hidden knowledge through the manipulation of objects, the interpretation of omens, or by the help of a supernatural power. Divination was divided into four groups. The first – astrology, enchanting, horoscope, and zodiac – are efforts to foretell people's personal, social, and business lives. The second – reading tarot cards, crystal balls, palms reading, rod and pendulum, and snail shells – is also an effort to look into the future. The third – numerology and dreams – tries to use numbers to interpret dreams and see what is ahead. The last group – telepathy, clairvoyance, clairaudience and psychometry – are attempts to learn hidden information about people or objects through extrasensory perception.

The second practice of the occult is 'Spiritism' or spiritualism, which is the attempt to communicate with spirits. Spiritualism believes that people can, by means of spiritualists, make contacts with the spirits of dead people who provide guidance for the living. Spiritism was classified into two necromancy, familiar spirits, mediums, séance, trumpet mediums (TM), ghosts, and phantoms. The second type included the consultation of other spirits, the use of Ouija Boards, automatic writing, and trance-speaking.

The third practice of the occult is sorcery and magic. Sorcery includes the use of drugs, charms, amulets, and appeals to supernatural powers. Magic is learning techniques and acquiring knowledge to perform signs and wonders through appeals to supernatural powers.

The final practice of the occult is witchcraft and astral projection. Though the term witchcraft was used in connection with sorcery and magic, I separated it and used it in connection with astral projection, because they are similar. The witch is one who was able to experience dissociation to cause good or evil; astral projection is known as out-of-body experience (OBE), and soul travel.

The term 'witchdemonology' describes the beliefs and practices of 'deliverance ministries' in Africa, which often combine traditional African beliefs about witches with Western Christian concepts of demonology and exorcism.

In Chapter Eleven, we saw that murder has taken on many faces in contemporary world. Serial killing was seen as a dangerous stronghold. Yet another growing murder was those who kill in a result of frustration. Still others might kill as a form of revenge or even contract others to kill on their behalf as a cover up.

In Chapter Twelve we saw that the devil is working under the guises of Satanism to deceive many; among them are the youth. Although advocates of Satanism may be people who don't believe in God or the devil, Satan uses it as a tool to deceive many from having the true knowledge of God.

Now we turn our attention to the weapons of our warfare in the following chapters.

PART FOUR

THE WEAPONS OF OUR
WARFARE

14

THE WEAPONS OF OUR STRUGGLE

In Part Three, we discussed the devil's schemes which are strongholds that he (the devil) has built into the day to day activities of human beings. These strongholds are in people's minds, and they block people from receiving the truth of the gospel of our Lord Jesus Christ. Thus, we say that the mind is the battleground in the contest between God and Satan.

The strongholds are so powerful that only divine power will break them. God through our Lord Jesus Christ has already broken the powers of the devil, and God has commissioned us to declare this so that people can be set free. How can we do this? We can do this effectively if we know what God has done for us in Christ. Secondly, we can do this if we know the weapons available to us, and we use them properly.

The rest of the book teaches about the weapons that are available to believers. The approach that I adopt here is pastoral; I present it in such a way that it will be useful for teaching in the church.

The battle has been identified as 'warfare', 'struggle', 'wrestle', or 'fight', and on the cross, Jesus completely defeated Satan and his evil powers in the heavenly realms, and we are seated with Christ (Eph. 1.3, 20; 2.6; 3.10). Our responsibility is to appropriate Jesus' victory in everyday life by faith. The knowledge of Scripture is absolutely essential in our Christian life; through it, we can make good use of God's weapons and provisions for our life.

The Scripture tells us about the weapons God has given us so that we can succeed in the struggle. We shall now examine them.

The full Armour of God (Ephesians 6.10-18).

[10] Finally, my brethren, be strong in the Lord, and in the power of his might. [11] Put on the whole armour of God, that ye may be able to stand against the wiles of the devil. [12] For we wrestle not against flesh and blood, but against principalities, against powers, against the rulers of the darkness of this world, against spiritual wickedness in high places. [13] Wherefore take unto you the whole armour of God, that ye may be able to withstand in the evil day, and having done all, to stand. [14] Stand therefore, having your loins girt about with truth, and having on the breastplate of righteousness; [15] And your feet shod with the preparation of the gospel of peace; [16] Above all, taking the shield of faith, wherewith ye shall be able to quench all the fiery darts of the wicked. [17] And take the helmet of salvation, and the sword of the Spirit, which is the word of God: [18] Praying always with all prayer and supplication in the Spirit, and watching thereunto with all perseverance and supplication for all saints; [19] And for me, that utterance may be given unto me, that I may open my mouth boldly, to make known the mystery of the gospel (Eph. 6.10-19, KJV).

Some Christians have divided the weapons here into two parts: the defensive and offensive. The defensive weapons are:

- The girt of truth; or belt of truth

- The breastplate of righteousness

- The shoes of the preparation of gospel of peace

- The shield of faith

- The helmet of salvation

- And the sword of the Spirit, the word of God.

The offensive weapons:

- The sword of the Spirit, the word of God

- Prayer.

The reason why some of the weapons are termed defensive is that they are mainly used to defend oneself from the enemy. The offensive ones are used to attack. I shall not stress the division between the defensive and the offensive, because the division gives the impression that we need so many weapons because the devil is strong. But that is not the real point. Paul was simply using the armour of a Roman soldier of his day to describe how well-equipped we are. The point is not the devil's strength but ours.

The armour of God listed here is not mystification but is simply an illustration of an accomplished work that God has done for us in Christ. Paul used this illustration because his readers would understand it. If he wrote it in our day, he might talk of bomb-proof, bullet proof, armoured plated, barricaded, ground-force attack, armoured attack, heavy bombardment, sea attack, tank assault, missile strike, rockets, bomb-dropping, high-level bombing, low-level bombing, armoured car, air raids, anti-aircraft artillery, and triple A.

The lesson that we can learn from this is what God has done for us in Christ. The illustration is not the point. Christ's work is the point. Paul's emphasis here is that you need to put on the full armour of God, so that you may be able to *stand* against the devil's schemes *when the day of evil* comes (Eph. 6.13, NIV). Take note that Paul says '*when* the day of evil comes' not *if* it comes. The day of evil will come. You need to put on the full armour of God, so that when the day of evil comes you will be prepared and not taken by surprise.

On the one hand, the armour of God is Jesus Christ himself. Once you put on Jesus, you have put on the full armour of God. He is all that we need in our Christian pilgrimage. On the other hand, if we say Jesus is all that we need, people won't fully understand what we mean. Therefore, Paul explains by illustration what Christ has done for us. The various descriptions of the armoury are to show believers what we have in Christ.

15

BELT OF TRUTH

The question that I asked myself when I started studying the weapons of our warfare was, 'Why is the belt of truth first on the list?' 'Stand therefore, having girded your waist with truth …' (Eph. 6.14, NKJV). Maybe Paul didn't mean anything significant by placing truth first, but truth is essential. If we examine truth as it is illustrated here, then, we can understand its importance.

During the time of Jesus and the Apostles, the normal clothing that people would put on was a loose type of garment as those put on by Muslims and some people in the Middle East. A soldier would have to tighten his girdle well so that it would not hinder his movement. A loosed girdle would certainly obstruct a good soldier at warfront.

Sincerity in Whatever We Do

Paul compares the girdle, which in our case is a belt, with truth. What is this in our daily Christian walk with God? This is sincerity, integrity, openness, frankness, and honesty. One of the texts that comes to mind when we speak on truth is Phil. 4.8, 'Finally, brethren, whatsoever things are true, whatsoever things are honest, whatsoever things are just, whatsoever things are pure, whatsoever things are lovely, whatsoever things are of good report; if there be any virtue, and if there be any praise, think on these things' (KJV). Christians are to be just in our daily activities and dealings with all sorts of people. Christians are to aim at things which will cause people around us to speak well and think well of us. We should do things that would attract applause from people around us. This is not to say that Christians should be seeking praise from people; rather it calls for being truthful in whatever situation and condition we find ourselves, in order for people around us to glorify the God we serve.

We are not right to move about with Pentecostal and Christian jargons, such as 'Brother I will pray for you', 'It was good', and 'That was great', – while we do not mean what we say. We need to be sincere. The devil can even pick on such loose words to attack the Christian.

If we are always truthful, we shall come out of every test and trial successfully; we shall not be accused or condemned by the devil unnecessarily. If what we do is morally and spiritually right, we shall not be afraid of the devil's threats and attacks. Satan himself will know that he will be fighting a lost battle.

Jesus is our Truth

The belt of truth we are discussing here is a weapon that can be used to protect believers from the onslaughts of the devil. The truth is Jesus. 'You say that I am a king, and you are right', Jesus said. 'I was born for that purpose. And I came to bring truth to the world. All who love the truth recognize that what I say is true' (Jn 18.37, NLT). Jesus makes it simple for his hearer at Jn 14.6, 'I am the way, the truth, and the life. No one can come to the Father except through me' (NLT). In other words, he is the one the prophets spoke about – the Messiah, He is the true manna, the true shepherd, the true tabernacle or temple of God, or simply put, he is the substance or reality of the Old Testament typologies, shadows and figures. He is truth, and truth is in Him. Whatever he says is final; he does not need revelation. He does not need the testimony from men. He is truth whether people believe in him or not. If you seek after the truth, you will find Jesus.

Jesus told his disciples, 'If you hold on to my teaching then you are really my disciples. Then you will know the truth and the truth will set you free' (Jn 8.31-32, NIV). On the contrary, he told the Pharisees that if God were their father they would believe in him, but they were of their father, the devil, who was the father of all lies (Jn 8.44).

The point that Jesus made here was that his genuine disciples are those who are, by the grace of God, rescued from the power of the father of lies, the devil, and receive the truth as taught by him. These people hear his voice and submit to his power and influence. They become his disciples, his subjects, who will bear faith in, and true allegiance to, him. Such people are set free from the deceit of the devil. They do not believe in the lies of Satan and his evil powers. They show no interest in myth and speculation, or expect extraordinary wisdom or power outside Jesus.

Belt of Truth Provides Confidence

If you put on Jesus and follow his teaching, you will have confidence in your Christian life. Nothing will frighten you. John writes:

> Dear Children, let us not love with words or tongues but with actions and in truth. This then is how we know that we belong to the truth, and how we set our hearts at rest in his presence whenever our hearts condemn us. For God is greater than our hearts, and he knows everything (1 Jn 3.18-20, NIV).

Once we are truthful in our daily lives, we put our hearts at rest in the presence of God and can endure the attacks of the devil. Some people are oversensitive to the point of having their hearts condemning them often; such people need to trust God to fulfil all his promises. He knows the hearts of everybody, their strength and weaknesses. Once you put on Jesus, he will make you willing and cause you to be truthful. He will certainly fulfil his part. Paul sums up, 'For no matter how many promises God has made, they are "Yes" in Christ. And so through him the "Amen" is spoken to the glory of God' (2 Cor. 1.20).

The Devil Knows the Truth

Put on the belt of truth to demonstrate that indeed you are a disciple of Jesus. The challenge is for you to obey the voice of the Holy Spirit and shun lies. Endeavour to come out from hypocrisy and display the character of Christ. Openness and frankness, no matter the situation, will shut up the devil. The devil knows the disciples of Jesus. A demon-possessed person told the seven sons of Sceva, 'Jesus I know, and I know Paul, but who are you?' (Acts 19.15, NIV). Here, it means the devil recognised Paul as a true disciple of Jesus. He respected Paul as a man who had the authority of Jesus. How does the devil know you?

The devil will know your identity but that will not deter him from tempting you or telling you lies. He will tell you lies to deceive you, but you need to put on the belt of truth, by telling the truth and trusting in the unfailing love of God to act on all what he has promised.

16

BREASTPLATE OF RIGHTEOUSNESS

The breastplate of righteousness is next on the list (Eph. 6.14). The breastplate covers the chest where the heart is. The breastplate of a soldier covers the heart, which is the most important organ of the body. In reference to the spiritual heart, Jesus said:

> For from within, *out of a person's heart*, come evil thoughts, sexual immorality, theft, murder, [22] adultery, greed, wickedness, deceit, eagerness for lustful pleasure, envy, slander, pride, and foolishness. [23] All these vile things come from within; they are what defile you and make you unacceptable to God' (Mk 7.21-23, NLT, italics mine).

'Out of a person's heart, come evil thoughts ...' (Mk 7.21). This makes the heart the centre of life. In Prov. 4.23, the wise man warns people, 'Guard your heart, for it is the wellspring of life' (NIV). What is in your heart will direct the course of your life, either for good or for evil. Paul admonishes Christians that we need the breastplate of righteousness to guard our hearts. What is it?

In 1 Thess. 5.8, Paul speaks about another breastplate: 'But let us, who are of the day, be sober, putting on the breastplate of faith and love; and for an helmet, the hope of salvation' (KJV). This time, he calls it a breastplate of faith and love. Why should he call it this way? First, it shows that the term breastplate was used as an illustration of what Christ has done for us. We need not make much noise about the illustration. The same can be used to explain other issues. Second, we can say that the breastplate of righteousness is also the breastplate of faith and love. In other words, the righteousness Paul speaks about here is something that you cannot earn as a Christian; it is something that comes by faith in Christ. In Rom. 1.17, Paul explains, 'For in it the righteousness of God is revealed from faith to faith; as it is written, "The just shall live by faith"' (NKJV). The faith that Paul speaks of here is to accept what God has done for humankind in Christ in faith. This righteousness comes from God on the basis of what God has done in Christ for us. Thus, in Phil. 3.9, we read, 'And be found in Him, not having my own righteousness, which *is* from the law, but that which *is* through faith in Christ, the righteousness which is from God by faith' (NJKV).

Why does God grant us this righteousness? The basis for granting this righteousness is God's love. Therefore, faith in Christ, which is the vehicle of receiving this righteousness, experiences the unfailing love of God (Rom. 5.5-8).

> [5] And this expectation will not disappoint us. For we know how dearly *God loves* us, because he has given us the Holy Spirit to fill our hearts with *his love.* [6] When we were utterly helpless, Christ came at just the right time and died for us sinners. [7] Now, no one is likely to die for a good person, though someone might be willing to die for a person who is especially good. [8] But God showed *his great love* for us by sending Christ to die for us while we were still sinners (NLT).

God has already demonstrated this to us, by sending Christ to die for us. Thus, it is a virtue that can never fail (1 Cor. 13.8). The Psalmist calls this virtue the 'unfailing love of God': 'Many are the woes of the wicked, but the Lord's unfailing love surrounds the man who trusts in him' (Ps. 32.10, NIV). 'I trust in God's unfailing love forever and ever' (Ps. 52.8). Nothing can separate us from this love; not even death (Rom. 8.38-39):

> [38] And I am convinced that nothing can ever separate us from his love. Death can't, and life can't. The angels can't, and the demons can't. Our fears for today, our worries about tomorrow, and even the powers of hell can't keep God's love away. [39] Whether we are high above the sky or in the deepest ocean, nothing in all creation will ever be able to separate us from the love of God that is revealed in Christ Jesus our Lord (NLT).

Paul prays for the Ephesians that they will understand how deep this unfailing love of God is (Eph. 3.17-18).

[17] And I pray that Christ will be more and more at home in your hearts as you trust in him. May your roots go down deep into the soil of God's marvelous love. [18] And may you have the power to understand, as all God's people should, how wide, how long, how high, and how deep his love really is. [19] May you experience the love of Christ, though it is so great you will never fully understand it. Then you will be filled with the fullness of life and power that comes from God (NLT).

Paul knew believers would never fully understand the depth of God's love. Yet, he knew having a glimpse of it was necessary for the full life and power of Christ to manifest itself in believers. Once sinners accept Christ, they are saved and delivered from the kingdom of Satan. The seed of righteousness is sown in them and they can live a righteous life. Yet, salvation will not stop the devil from attacking the believer with his deceits. Satan and his evil powers will continue to rob believers of their rights and privileges until they have clear knowledge of what God has done for them, hence Paul's prayer for understanding. Once you realize what God has done for you in Christ through his love and accept it by faith, you become righteous in Christ and begin to exhibit that life. Through our lives, we then grow in our understanding and knowledge of God's love.

If we consider what Jesus said, 'For from within, *out of a person's heart*, come ...' (Mk 7.21, NLT), then, once the seed of righteousness is planted in the believer, he/she will begin to desire for righteousness and live it. As we express the righteousness of Christ in our lives, people will know the sort of persons we are.

[16] You can detect them by the way they act, just as you can identify a tree by its fruit. You don't pick grapes from thornbushes, or figs from thistles. [17] A healthy tree produces good fruit, and an unhealthy tree produces bad fruit. [18] A good tree can't produce bad fruit, and a bad tree can't produce good fruit. [19] So every tree that does not produce good fruit is chopped down and thrown into the fire. [20] Yes, the way to identify a tree or a person is by the kind of fruit that is produced (Mt. 7.16-20, NLT).

The fruit which Jesus speaks about is obeying God's Word. This is what God expects from believers. The devil is shut up when believers are obedient to Christ. But this is not always the situation. Believers may fall below what the Word of God instructs and grieve the Holy Spirit who will never cease to convict believers. Such believers will have to repent and confess. If the devil continues to accuse, apply the breastplate of righteousness. The breastplate covers your heart from all onslaughts of the devil. This breastplate is there for your protection. Your responsibility is to accept it by faith, and you will enjoy your Christian life.

17

THE SHOES OF THE GOSPEL OF PEACE

One of the reasons Paul reminds Christians to put on the whole armour of God is that once we attack the devil, he will also attack back. His attacks come in different forms. If the soldier of Christ does not know the content of his message, he is likely to be deceived by the opponent. Therefore, Paul instructs believers to put on the shoes of the gospel of peace (Eph. 6.15).

The purpose of soldiers putting on a pair of strong shoes is to make their travels easy and to protect their feet as they move along. Paul calls the gospel, 'The preparation of the gospel of peace'. Christians must know the gospel, understand it, and apply it before they can effectively communicate it. It is the gospel of peace. But how can you communicate peace to others if you do not have it yourself or even understand what you are to say? The bare truth is that you can learn it, memorise it, teach it but if you do not experience it, you cannot transmit peace to others.

The message of the gospel is indeed peace. The prophet Isaiah prophesied of the messenger who ran from the battle scene to bring good news of the defeat of the enemy. The deliverance that has been brought by the king can rightly be applied to those who proclaim the gospel, 'How beautiful on the mountains are the feet of those who bring good news, who proclaim peace, who bring good tidings, who proclaim salvation, who say to Zion, Your God reigns' (Isa. 52.7 NIV).

Jesus commissioned the disciples, 'As you enter a home … let your peace rest on it; if it is not, let your peace return to you' (Mt. 10.12-13, NIV). The New Living Translation brings a new insight into the peace we leave with people, 'When you are invited into someone's home, give it your blessing. If it turns out to be a worthy home, let your blessing stand; if it is not, take back the blessing.' This means 'the peace' we are to leave with the people is 'the blessing of God' in our lives. This is the gospel. If you don't have the gospel, you cannot give it out. If you have it and give it out and they don't like it, you take it back.

In Jesus we have our peace; he is our peace. Jesus declares, 'I am leaving you with a gift – peace of mind and heart. And the peace I give isn't like the peace the world gives. So don't be troubled or afraid (Jn 14.27, NLT). Again in Jn 16.33, Jesus says, 'I have told you all this so that you may have peace in me. Here on earth you will have many trials and sorrows. But take heart, because I have overcome the world' (NLT). The gospel of our Lord Jesus carries peace with it, because in it, we are justified. 'Therefore, since we have been made right in God's sight by faith, we have peace with God because of what Jesus Christ our Lord has done for us' (Rom. 5.1). The gospel is good news indeed. In it, the sinner has been made right with God. Everybody is invited no matter how sinful the person is.

Nevertheless, without preparation you will not be able to communicate the gospel message well. A soldier must put the shoes on before moving safely around in his work. What is this preparation? Preparation is the study and the knowledge of the Scripture, especially the clear understanding of the gospel. Without understanding of the gospel, the proclaiming believer can easily be deceived. Remind yourself that the devil knows the Scripture, and he used it to tempt the Lord Jesus Christ. Our study of the false doctrines has also shown that some false teachers started well until they were deceived.[119] The implication is that if you do not prepare as a good soldier of Christ, you can be deceived. Therefore, preparation is very important for you to know clearly what God has done for you, what you have and then give it to others.

I know a certain brother in Christ, who made a fool of himself as he attempted to preach to some non-Christian friends. One of the friends annoyed him, to the point that my Christian brother

---

[119] See Chapter Six for discussion of false doctrines.

took a knife and threatened to stab him. The other friends prevented him. He was not prepared.

Preparation also includes the ability to communicate the gospel. The soldier of Christ should know the gospel and have the ability to communicate it. You must know the gospel and present it in a simple way that brings peace to people. Lack of clear knowledge of the gospel and clarity of preparation has produced shallow Christians. Such Christians do not have peace of mind. In some cases, some of these people become more wretched once they become Christians, because they have not indeed received the gospel of peace. The gospel must produce peace, for it is the gospel of peace.

Do you really have peace in Christ? Do you understand your salvation? Do you know the power that the death of Christ and his resurrection have brought to you? Do you know that you are secured? You will certainly have peace if you understand the work that God has done for you in Christ.

18

THE SHIELD OF FAITH

The fourth weapon is the shield of faith. The shield that Paul speaks about here was a long rectangular shield. The good soldier could use it to protect his whole body. When we attack the devil we can be sure that he will also counterattack. He uses schemes, deceits, and lies. Often, he first attacks the mind. All sorts of foolish ideas, thoughts, desires, and options come to mind. If he fails to get you, he may attack your closest neighbour, your wife, husband, child, friend, or a family member who is under your authority. As a leader, for example, the devil may attack a member of your church. This is the time that you must apply the shield of faith.

We have already found out that the breastplate of righteousness is also called the breastplate of faith and love. There is a difference between the breastplate of faith and love and the shield of faith. The breastplate of faith and love is used as a personal protection when the devil accuses. When the devil attacks, you appropriate the righteousness of God through faith for yourself. The shield of faith, however, is the faith which can be used to protect yourself and those whom the Lord has committed to your care or those around you.

David, an Old Testament saint, often used the shield of faith. Examine the words he told the priest Abiathar, 'Stay with me; don't be afraid; the man who is seeking your life is seeking mine also. *You will be safe with me*' (1 Sam. 22.23, emphasis mine). This is the man who knows whom he believes; the one who does not panic when the devil strikes. He knows the Lord will protect and provide. He knows deep within him that the Lord is with him, and he is secure.

This is what we call the presence of God with people. Although Saul wanted to him kill him and moved the whole army of Israel against David, yet because the Lord was with David, he knew he was not only very safe but those who were with him were all safe.

When I was conducting research on witchcraft, I interviewed self-claimed witches, demon-possessed people, sorcerers, traditional priests/priestesses, and alleged former witches, sorcerers, and demon possessed people. Sometimes I went with personal assistants who took notes for me because some of them did not like their interviews to be recorded. On one occasion, one of the assistants mentioned to me that he was very much afraid during the interview. In fact after one of the interviews, he said he saw a snake when going to the house. After he had entered the room, he saw another one. According to him, he had never experienced anything like that before. I told him that with me around he would be safe. I was not boasting, but I knew the God I served, and I knew clearly without a doubt that the devil could not hurt him, without seeking permission from God. I knew that God wanted me to do the job I was doing, and thus he would supply all the resources I needed, and he would protect all the people who were working with me.

The devil may move the whole force of his kingdom – principalities, rulers, powers of this dark world, spiritual wickedness in the heavenly realms – against you, but with God on your side, you are very safe. Oh, how I wish this would sink deeply into your spirit and soul as a Christian.

Earlier on David had used this shield of faith to deliver the whole of Israel from the devil's slavery. He told King Saul:

> But David persisted. 'I have been taking care of my father's sheep', he said. 'When a lion or a bear comes to steal a lamb from the flock, I go after it with a club and take the lamb from its mouth. If the animal turns on me, I catch it by the jaw and club it to death. I have done this to both lions and bears, and I'll do it to this pagan Philistine, too, *for he has defied the armies of the living God!* The Lord who saved me from the claws of the lion and the bear will save me from this Philistine!' Saul finally consented. 'All right, go ahead', he said. 'And may the Lord be with you!' (1 Sam. 17.34-37, NLT, italics mine).

This is the shield of faith. It is not a physical weapon. The weapons we fight with are not of the world. King Saul nearly made this mistake. Whereas David was talking about spiritual weapons, Saul was thinking of physical weapons. Thus, he freely offered David physical weapons. Read on:

> Then Saul gave David his own armor – a bronze helmet and a coat of mail. David put it on, strapped the sword over it, and took a step or two to see what it was like, for he had never worn such things before. 'I can't go in these', he protested. 'I'm not used to them.' So he took them off again. He picked up five smooth stones from a stream and put them in his shepherd's bag. Then, armed only with his shepherd's staff and sling, he started across to fight Goliath (1 Sam. 17.38-40, NLT).

David wisely rejected those weapons and went along to fight in the usual way he killed the lions and the bears. Champions often do not rely on other people's weapons. They do things in their own way; their methods are often different from the norm. They don't purposely decide to be different, they just see the challenge from a different angle. Often what they see is the real issue. Thus, their actions become the solutions. Who will believe a soldier going to war without having the required armour? David knew the battle was between God and Satan. Once Satan had already lost the battle, he needed to fight behind God who was already victorious. God was his shield of faith.

The shield of faith we are talking about is not a matter of taking a physical shield to protect yourself, neither is it like taking a sword to strike the devil. It is not just a matter of declaring, 'I claim the shield of faith!' It is faith in Jesus, the Captain who has defeated the devil for you. Faith in him is the shield. You do not need any special techniques, but worship God in the usual way just as you do, and put your trust in him. Putting your trust in his Word as the truth from God, and believing all what he has said in his Word, the Bible, is the faith that will protect you from the devil's snares and deceits.

David knew that Goliath was the agent of the devil because he defied the armies of the Lord. This was what bothered David. Goliath, an uncircumcised person, that is, an unbeliever, could not defy the armies of the living God. David, therefore, knew the battle was the Lord's. Examine the text quoted above critically; David did not even pray. He was already a man of the Holy Spirit because he often prayed and worshiped the Lord. Prayer, praise, and shepherding the flock were his routine business. He was already strong in the Lord and his mighty power. The Lord was already with him. Accordingly, he went to face this possessed demonic agent who was physically well built and trained. David was able to kill him in the name of the Lord God Almighty (1 Sam. 17.45). Yes, this was the shield of faith which led to the protection and deliverance of a whole nation. John declares, 'For every child of God defeats this evil world by trusting Christ to give the victory. And the ones who win this battle against the world are the ones who believe that Jesus is the Son of God' (1 Jn 5.4-5, NLT). The New International Version reads, 'For everyone born of God overcomes the world. This is the victory that has overcome the world, even our faith' (1 Jn 5.4).

Are the people around you protected? Do you give them a covering?

19

THE HELMET OF SALVATION

Another important weapon that Paul mentions is the helmet of Salvation. 'Put on salvation as your helmet' (Eph. 6.17, NLT). The New King James Version puts it this way, 'And take the helmet of salvation'. A helmet is worn on the head. The purpose is to protect the brain from any injury. The brain is the seat of the mind, and the mind controls what people do. The mind directs the affairs of people. A sound mind is a good health. An insane mind negatively affects the movement of a person. Putting on salvation as a helmet is to instruct you to hold on to salvation as the anchor of your Christian life. Wrong understanding of salvation will negatively affect your Christian life. You can be blown up by every wave of the devil. Things may not be done in the right perspective. It is not surprising therefore that many Christians are out of balance now. The reason is that they have not put on salvation as a helmet.

The helmet of salvation was first mentioned in Isa. 59.17 in the context of the work of the Messiah. 'For he put on righteousness as a breastplate, and an helmet of salvation upon his head; and he put on the garments of vengeance *for* clothing, and was clad with zeal as a cloak' (KJV). Here salvation was the helmet that the Lord wore in battle. In this case, the helmet of salvation stands for God's determination and power to save those for whom he fights. Nothing can change what he plans to do. It is decreed, sanctioned and secured. He puts on the helmet of salvation.

In 1 Thess. 5.8, Paul throws more light on what he means by the helmet of salvation. 'But let us who are of the day be sober, putting on the breastplate of faith and love, and *as* a helmet the hope of salvation' (NJKV). Here, we realise that the helmet that Paul talks about is the hope of salvation. We believe with our hearts unto salvation, but we need hope to continue in our Christian lives. We have already established the fact that the battleground of the devil is the mind of people. The devil uses schemes and doubts to attack the certainty of a Christian's salvation. If Christians are sure and hopeful about their salvation, the devil loses a very important aspect of the battle.

Now, let us try to link Isaiah with 1 Thessalonians. In Isaiah, the helmet was God's determination and power to save people. Nothing can thwart what God has planned to do; it is certain and secured. Paul's exhortation for believers in Thessalonians is that they should put on this helmet, which gives them the assurance and security that what God has provided for them (salvation) is real and secured. Nothing can change it. They must be hopeful about their salvation.

Hope and faith are linked together. 'Now faith is the substance of things hoped for, the evidence of things not seen' (NKJ). The New Living Translation is clearer here, 'What is faith? It is the confident assurance that what we hope for is going to happen. It is the evidence of things we cannot yet see' (Heb. 11.1).

Faith is the ground on which hope is built. This means that if we have solid faith, we have solid hope. If our belief is presumptuous, our hope will also be illusive. But if we have a sure and solid foundation for our faith, then we can also build a solid hope that will be the helmet for the protection for our mind and thinking.

Apart from Christ, a person has no hope:

In those days you were living apart from Christ. You were excluded from God's people, Israel, and you did not know the promises God had made to them. You lived in this world without God and without hope. But now you belong to Christ Jesus. Though you once were far away from God, now you have been brought near to him because of the blood of Christ (Eph. 2.12-13, NLT).

The hope that Christians have is that Jesus will complete what He has begun. He has taken us as his own and put his Spirit in us as a seal. 2 Corinthians 1.20-22 states this:

For all the promises of God in Him *are* Yes, and in Him Amen, to the glory of God through us. Now He who establishes us with you in Christ and has anointed us *is* God, who also has sealed us and given us the Spirit in our hearts as a guarantee (NKJV).

By this, Paul explains that God has placed the Holy Spirit in our hearts as an assurance that we are his own and that what he has said, he will fulfil. This should make Christians stand firm for Christ. This is our hope. The Holy Spirit in us means Christ is in us. Therefore, Christ in the believer is the hope of glory (Col. 1.27).

The Epistle of Hebrews brings out a very solid foundation of hope.

> For men indeed swear by the greater, and an oath for confirmation *is* for them an end of all dispute. Thus God, determining to show more abundantly to the heirs of promise the immutability of His counsel, confirmed *it* by an oath, that by two immutable things, in which it *is* impossible for God to lie, we might have strong consolation, who have fled for refuge to lay hold of the hope set before *us*. This *hope* we have as an anchor of the soul, both sure and steadfast, and which enters the *Presence* behind the veil, where the forerunner has entered for us, *even* Jesus, having become High Priest forever according to the order of Melchizedek (Heb. 6.16-20, NKJV).

The writer of Hebrews gives us two very strong grounds on which the Christian's hope is built. These are first the very nature of God, and second his oath. God's promises, unlike human beings, are all founded in his eternal counsel, which is unchangeable. This is to say that God planned our salvation from the beginning of the world; it was not a rash and hasty decision, since he does not need to change what he says. This is what theologians mean when they say that God's nature is immutable. Nothing new can appear to God, because he sees the end from the beginning. He knows everything at once. God's purpose of salvation was agreed upon in counsel, and settled there among the Father, Son, and Holy Spirit.

In this text, the writer shows us these two unchangeable things which make our hope very strong. First, God has given us his promise (counsel), and second he has given us his oath. Our hope of salvation is very secure since it is impossible for God to lie, contrary to his nature as well as to his will.

Then the writer gives us two illustrations to drive home his message. The first illustration is an indirect reference to the altar of God in the Old Covenant. This is seen in the passage, 'We might have strong consolation, who have fled for refuge to lay hold of the hope set before *us*' (Heb. 6.18b, NKJV). Bringing in the phrase 'fled for refuge to lay hold of' brings our attention to the Old Covenant, where the altar at the temple was used as a place of refuge. The altar was used as protection for those who had killed and were being pursued to be killed. Such people could flee to get hold of the horns of the altar for safety. Again, in the Old Covenant, there were cities of refuge provided for those who were pursued by the avenger of blood. Those people could go for safety in the city of refuge.

In the Old Covenant people could overlook this protection. An example of this was the execution of Joab:

> Although he had not followed Absalom earlier, Joab had also joined Adonijah's revolt. When Joab heard about Adonijah's death, he ran to the sacred tent of the LORD and caught hold of the horns of the altar. [29] When news of this reached King Solomon, he sent Benaiah son of Jehoiada to execute him. [30]Benaiah went into the sacred tent of the LORD and said to Joab, 'The king orders you to come out!' But Joab answered, 'No, I will die here.' So Benaiah returned to the king and told him what Joab had said. [31] 'Do as he said', the king replied. 'Kill him there beside the altar and bury him. This will remove the guilt of his senseless murders from me and from my father's family' … [34] So Benaiah son of Jehoiada returned to the sacred tent and killed Joab, and Joab was buried at his home in the wilderness (1 Kgs 2.28-34, NLT).

Joab was killed despite the fact that he went to the sacred tent and caught hold of the horns of the altar. There was no safety for him.

Here, the writer of Hebrews says that when all the pressures are against you and you appear helpless, flee to get hold of the heavenly altar which has pacified our souls through the death of Christ. His promise is eternal, and it can never be changed. In God's provision of salvation in Christ is a much better city of refuge prepared by the gospel, a refuge for all sinners who shall have the heart to flee to it.

The second illustration of hope is an anchor. An anchor is a heavy piece of metal attached to a ship or boat by a cable and cast overboard to hold it in a particular place by means of a fluke that digs into the bottom. Here, the writer shows that the '*hope* we have as an anchor of the soul is both sure and steadfast, and it enters the *Presence* behind the veil' (Heb. 6.19, NKJ). He sees believers as we are in this world as a ship at sea, liable to be tossed up and down, and in danger of being cast away. The temptations, sufferings, misfortunes, persecutions, and afflictions that we go through are like the winds and waves that threaten shipwreck. We are in continual danger of being crushed or destroyed, so we need an anchor to keep us sure and steady.

The anchor that will protect is our hope of salvation in Christ. This anchor is steadfast in the sense that it is cast upon the rock, which is the Rock of Ages. It does not seek to fasten in the sands, but enters within the veil, and fixes there upon Christ. He is the hold of the believer's hope. Jesus Christ, and his work, is the object and ground of the believer's hope. This hope is solid. The reasons are that first, he has entered within the veil, to make a sacrifice of himself for us and proceeded to intercede for us before God. Second, he has gone within the veil as a forerunner to prepare a place for us, and to assure us that we shall follow him. Thus, he is the first fruits of believers, both in his resurrection and in his ascension. Third, Jesus is a permanent high priest after the order of Melchisedec. His priesthood will never cease, never fail, till he has accomplished his whole work.

This is the hope of salvation that the writer of Hebrews presents. It is like a helmet that should protect us.

Paul therefore hammers the message home by saying, 'And take the helmet of salvation' (Eph. 6.17, NKJV). The use of the term 'take' from the Greek *dechomai* is very important. *Dechomai* literally means 'receive'. Paul had earlier used the term 'put on' for the other pieces of armour. To change the expression 'put on' to 'take' or 'receive' is to give the impression that salvation is a gift given to us by God. We need to accept it, receive it, and live by it.

Christians must make salvation our hope. This good hope, through grace, of eternal life, will be a spiritual helmet to defend the head, and prevent the devil from winning over our minds through his schemes.

20

THE SWORD OF THE SPIRIT

The next weapon that Paul mentions is the sword of the Spirit. Paul makes it very easy for Christians to understand what he means; '… and take the sword of the Spirit, which is the word of God' (Eph. 6.17). This means the sword of the Spirit is the word of God. Physically the sword can be used to defend as well as to attack. It is therefore a very important weapon. Among the illustrative weapons that Paul presented in Ephesians, this is the main weapon of attack against the devil's strongholds.

The Sword of the Spirit as Double-edged Sword

The Bible teaches that the Word of God is like a double-edged sword; in other words a weapon that can be used for defense and offense in our struggle with the devil. The first biblical reference to look at is Heb. 4.12:

> For the word of God *is* living and powerful, and sharper than any two-edged sword, piercing even to the division of soul and spirit, and of joints and marrow, and is a discerner of the thoughts and intents of the heart (NJKV).

Here, the Scriptures show that the Word of God is powerful and living. The 'word' to which the writer is referring is the written Word of God, or the recorded word that God has already spoken. We must not think that the written word is inactive. It is alive and penetrates to the deepest part of a human being. In order for the writer to explain how effective and active the word of God is, he compares it with a double-edged sword. It is sharper than any two-edged sword; it cuts through the joints and marrows or our inner-most desires. No wonder some people sometimes put the written word of God under their pillows and sleep on it. The Word of God is indeed powerful. However, the concern of the writer here is not just placing the Word under a pillow or holding it in your hands, but the acceptance and application of the Word that makes it what it is meant to be. God's Word will confront, convict and cause to happen whatever God has purposed.

Next we will consider a group of texts taken from Rev. 1.16; 2.12, 16:

> He held seven stars in his right hand, and a sharp two-edged sword came from his mouth. And his face was as bright as the sun in all its brilliance (NLT).

> Write this letter to the angel of the church in Pergamum. This is the message from the one who has a sharp two-edged sword (NLT).

> Repent, or I will come to you suddenly and fight against them with the sword of my mouth (NLT).

All the three texts show that the Word of God is like a sharp sword, which means it is sharp, powerful, cuts across, and accomplishes whatever God purposes it to do.

The last text is taken from Isa. 49.1-2, 6:

> Listen to me, all of you in far-off lands! The LORD called me before my birth; from within the womb he called me by name. [2] He made my words of judgment as sharp as a sword. He has hidden me in the shadow of his hand. I am like a sharp arrow in his quiver ... [6] He says, 'You will do more than restore the people of Israel to me. I will make you a light to the Gentiles, and you will bring my salvation to the ends of the earth' (NLT).

Here, Isaiah prophesies about the Saviour of the world, the Messiah. He indicates that God has made his mouth like a sharp sword or a very sharp arrow. This is a picture of battle. The Messiah was to fight God's battle against the powers of darkness: '... I will make you a light for the Gentiles, and you will bring my salvation to the ends of the earth' (Isa. 49.6, NLT). He was to fight and conquer the devil and bring the Gentiles to the Lord; he was also to bring God's people, Israel, back to him. He was to do this through the sharp sword, the Word of the Lord that has been placed in his mouth. This shows us that the Word of God is the greatest weapon we can use against the devil. It can be used to destroy the works of the devil as well as to redeem people.

Now I want us to look at the word of God as a defensive weapon.

The Sword of the Spirit as a Defensive Weapon

The sword of the Spirit as a defensive weapon is well described in the confrontation between Satan and Jesus at Mt. 4.1-11 and Lk. 4.1-13.[120]

> [1] Then Jesus was led up by the Spirit into the wilderness to be tempted by the devil. [2] And when He had fasted forty days and forty nights, afterward He was hungry. [3] Now when the tempter came to Him, he said, '*If You are the Son of God*, command that these stones become bread.' [4] But He answered and said, '*It is written*, "Man shall not live by bread alone, but by every word that proceeds from the mouth of God".' [5] Then the devil took Him up into the holy city, set Him on the pinnacle of the temple, [6] and said to Him, '*If You are the Son of God*, throw Yourself down. For it is written: "He shall give His angels charge over you", and, "In *their* hands they shall bear you up, Lest you dash your foot against a stone."' [7] Jesus said to him, '*It is written again*, "You shall not tempt the LORD your God".' [8] Again, the devil took Him up on an exceedingly high mountain, and showed Him all the kingdoms of the world and their glory. [9] And he said to Him, 'All these things I will give You *if You will fall down and worship me*'. [10] Then Jesus said to him, 'Away with you, Satan! For *it is written*, "You shall worship the LORD your God, and Him only you shall serve".' [11] Then the devil left Him, and behold, angels came and ministered to Him (Mt. 4.1-11, NKJV, Italic mine).

---

[120] See Chapter Five for the discussion of the temptation.

We realise that here Satan directly attacked the Son of God and tried to fill Jesus' mind with doubts. The battleground is always the mind. In all three temptations, he began with the conjunction 'if' ('If you are the Son of God ...' Mt. 4.3, 6; Lk. 4.3, 9). The conjunction 'if' is to cause a question about what has been said or done already. What had been said or done already? The devil was basing his temptation on the voice that came out during the baptism of Jesus. 'This is my Son, whom I love, with him I am well pleased' (Mt. 3.17, NIV). The devil was saying, 'You are not the Son of God. If you are then tell these stones to become bread' (Mt. 4.3, NIV). He wanted Jesus to doubt the Word of God. This is the battle in the mind. Once Satan gains the mind, he can cause major confusion.

Jesus answers with the sword of the Spirit, which is the Word of God. 'It is written.' This tells us the importance of knowing, understanding and applying the Word of God in our particular situations. Jesus had fasted and prayed for forty days, but the devil came to tempt. This is an indication that no matter what you do as a Christian, the devil will tempt you. Prayer and fasting will not stop him from tempting you. Paul is right in emphasising, 'And after you have done everything, to stand' (Eph. 6.13). We stand on the Word of God, and use it as the sword of the Spirit against the devil. The Word of God is not just like a double-edged sword, but sharper than any double edged sword (Heb. 4.12). It is active and a living power that accomplishes the purposes for which it is meant.

The devil did not question the power of the Word; He recognized the power of the Scriptures but misquoted them. This is significant for Christians. Many false doctrines have arisen because the devil successfully won the minds of people through the misapplication of the Word of God. Others also have fallen into serious vices because the devil was able to corrupt their minds with the misapplication of the Scriptures. We must understand the simple Word of God and apply it correctly. This is not necessarily a call for you to leave your work to study theology and defend doctrine, but it is a call for you to understand the basic truths of the Bible and to use the Word daily in your Christian life. Reading the Bible daily will help you to understand it. Jesus did not provide the devil with a long theological discourse; he simply quoted the written Word of God.

Jesus didn't tire of using the word of God against the devil. In all three temptations, he simply said, 'It is written' (Mt. 4:4, 7, 10). This informs us about the need to always turn to the Word of God. There is no need to seek for new revelations or special encounters when we are facing the devil; God will give us revelations when we need them. The truth is that God has already given us the solution to the devil; it is God's Word. Leaning on it at the time of hardship will always work. You cannot successfully handle the devil without knowing the Scriptures. You must know, memorise, understand, accept, and apply them. It works.

Read on to learn more about the Word of God as the powerful weapon that demolishes the strongholds of the devil.

21

THE MINISTRY OF THE WORD OF GOD

Preaching and teaching are what I am referring to here as the ministry of the Word, which is the sword of the Spirit. The ministry of the Word is another aspect of the Spirit which is a powerful and destructive instrument used to demolish the strongholds of the devil. Whenever the Word is truly ministered, the devil will always react.

Satan Cannot Stand Against the Power of the Word in the Church

Jesus predicted Satan's reaction to the power of the gospel to his apostle in Matthew:

> Simon Peter answered, 'You are the Messiah, the Son of the living God'. Jesus replied, 'You are blessed, Simon son of John, because my Father in heaven has revealed this to you. You did not learn this from any human being. Now I say to you that you are Peter, and upon this rock I will build my church, and all the powers of hell will not conquer it. And I will give you the keys of the Kingdom of Heaven. Whatever you lock on earth will be locked in heaven, and whatever you open on earth will be opened in heaven' (Mt. 16.16-19, NLT).

Here Jesus tells about the offensive nature of the church. The information is that Jesus was going to build his church upon the rock of Peter's confession, 'You are the Messiah, the Son of the living God'. He would build the church, but Peter and his friends were

not going to be left out, he was going to do it through them, because whatever they 'lock on earth will be locked in heaven'. Power
has been given to them to do the work on behalf of Christ. The
power is the proclamation of the gospel. That is, power flows
through the preaching of the gospel; this is the declaration that Jesus is the Son of God. The preaching of the gospel is the power
that demolishes the stronghold of the devil. The church is established when the Gospel is preached. Satan's power cannot withstand it. This is evident in the statement of Jesus, 'I will build my
church, and the *gates* of *Hades* shall not prevail against it' (Mt. 16.18,
NKJV).

The term '*Hades*' in the New King James Version is what the
New Living Translation translates as Hell. The 'power of Hell cannot conquer it' means Satan cannot overcome it. The Greek term
for hell here is *hades,* which literally means 'unseen'; that is, the unseen place of the departed souls. Hades represents the unseen kingdom of the devil. The passage therefore teaches that in the course
of delivering the message of the Gospel, the devil will try to defend
himself, but his power cannot overcome the strength of the Word.

Another term to consider is 'power' in the New Living Translation and 'gate' in the New King James Version. In the Old Testament, the gate was the place where the ruling council of elders met
to judge and make decisions. It was also the town hall for the normal business and legal transactions, where witnesses were always
available (Prov. 31.23; Ruth 4.1).

Normally if the enemy is attacking, he will attack the gates because the gate leads to the city. If the enemy will attack through the
gate, then the gate should be fortified. Fortifying the gate implies
that the most deadly and powerful weapons will be placed at the
gate; fighting happens at the gate. Isaiah gives a picture of this:

> He will give a longing for justice to your judges and great cour-
> age to your soldiers who are battling to the last before your gates
> (Isa. 28.6, LB).

> For a spirit of justice to him who sits in judgment, And for
> strength to those who turn back the battle at the gate (Isa. 28.6,
> NKJV).

Here Isaiah is saying that the Lord will give courage and strength
to the soldiers who fight the enemy at the gate. God gives his peo-

ple the requisite courage and the boldness to carry out their duties in the midst of the difficulties and oppositions they are likely to meet. The strength will be given whether they are defending their own gates or attacking the gates of another. The strength of the army depends upon God's justice, wisdom, and power.

Now, coming back to Mt. 16.18, the picture that Jesus, therefore, gives is that the Church will move to the devil's territory through the proclamation of the message that Jesus is the Son of God, and all the powers (gates) of the devil will not be able to stand against it. This calls for the preaching of the Word; it is the power of God that destroys the stronghold of the devil.

Preaching the Word is a Charge

Preaching the Word is a mighty weapon against Satan's strongholds. Accordingly, Paul instructs Timothy to preach the word in season and out of season.

> And so I solemnly urge you before God and before Christ Jesus – who will someday judge the living and the dead when he appears to set up his Kingdom: [2] Preach the word of God. Be persistent, whether the time is favorable or not. Patiently correct, rebuke, and encourage your people with good teaching. [3] For a time is coming when people will no longer listen to right teaching. They will follow their own desires and will look for teachers who will tell them whatever they want to hear. [4] They will reject the truth and follow strange myths. [5] But you should keep a clear mind in every situation. Don't be afraid of suffering for the Lord. Work at bringing others to Christ. Complete the ministry God has given you (2 Tim. 4.1-4, NLT).

This was a solemn charge; one of the greatest commands that has ever been given in the Bible. The charge is to preach the Word. The reference to God who will judge people is to remind the preacher that he is accountable to God for whatever he preaches. Why is this reminder important? The reason is that a time is coming when people will not like to hear God's Word but will hear what they want to hear. In fact this has always been the case. The prophet Micah declared, 'Suppose a prophet full of lies were to say to you, "I'll preach to you the joys of wine and drink!" That's just the kind of prophet you would like!' (Mic. 2.11, NLT).[121] Even in Micah's generation people didn't always want to hear God's Word. This also means not all people will receive the truth. Therefore, those who preach the Word will face persecution and troubles, but they should still maintain their focus and preach the word.

Jesus commanded his apostles to 'go and make disciples of all nations' (Mt. 28.19, NIV), and this includes preaching and teaching (Mt. 28.20).

Why is preaching the Word important? The point has already been established that there is power in the Word of God. The power in the Word can demolish strongholds of Satan. When Peter was released from prison through divine intervention, he was instructed by the angel, 'Go, stand in the temple court … and tell the people the full message of this new life' (Acts 5.20, NIV). Since the angels could not preach the gospel, the charge given to Peter was to go and preach the full message. There is no substitute to the preaching of the Word. The gospel is the power of God for the salvation to all who believe (Rom. 1.16).

Paul's Ministry is an Example of the Power of the Preached Word

The description of the ministry of Paul in Ephesus is an example of the great power that is within the Word of God. Paul preached the full Gospel.

> Then Paul went to the synagogue and *preached boldly* for the next three months, *arguing persuasively* about the Kingdom of God. [9]But some rejected his message and publicly spoke against the Way, so Paul left the synagogue and took the believers with him. Then he began *preaching daily* at the lecture hall of Tyrannus. [10]This went on for the next two years, so that people throughout the province of Asia – both Jews and Greeks – heard the Lord's message (Acts. 19.8-10, NLT, italics mine).

Paul preached the word consistently and convincingly for two years. The message was about the Kingdom of God. His preaching was so intensive and extensive that the Word went throughout the

---

[121] I discovered this scripture today (20/07/07) during my morning devotion.

entire province of Asia. The preaching of the Word must explain and apply the simple gospel of our Lord and what he has done for people. It should be preached daily; nothing should be substituted in its place.

Healing and Miracles

Luke, who wrote the book of Acts, shows the result of the preaching of the Word, 'God did extraordinary miracles through Paul, so that even handkerchiefs and aprons that had touched him were taken to the sick, and their illnesses were cured and the evil spirits left them' (Acts 19.11-12). I wonder why Luke uses the term 'extraordinary' here, because miracles are miracles. It is apparent that he wanted to lay emphasis on the fact that by preaching the word of God in the province, God performed extraordinary miracles. The Lord confirms his word with signs and wonders. Here again the emphasis is on 'God' who did the unusual miracles. God, not Paul, did the miracles. The role of Paul was to preach the Gospel. Believers are not to seek after or advertise for miracles. Miracles follow believers as they preach the Word (Mk 16.17).

Demons Cast Out, Strongholds Demolished

When Paul preached the Gospel evil spirits were also cast out of people. Paul was physically not present at some of the miracles that took place. Acts records that handkerchiefs and aprons that had touched him were sent to people and evil spirits were cast out. Again, this shows that God, through his people, is the one who casts out evil spirits. Paul was not there even to speak to evil spirits to come out. The presence of God, symbolised with Paul's handkerchief or apron, was enough to do the work. The preaching of the full Gospel liberates people from the shackles of Satan.

Satan's secrets were revealed as an evil spirit acknowledged the ministry of Paul in Ephesus. The story is interesting:

A team of Jews who were travelling from town to town casting out evil spirits tried to use the name of the Lord Jesus. The incantation they used was this: 'I command you by Jesus, whom Paul preaches, to come out!' [14] Seven sons of Sceva, a leading priest, were doing this. [15] But when they tried it on a man possessed by an evil spirit, the spirit replied, 'I know Jesus, and I know Paul. But who are you?' [16] And he leaped on them and attacked them with such violence that they fled from the house, naked and badly injured (Acts 19.13-16, NLT).

The story reveals that demons do not just go out at the command of the name of Jesus. The person who speaks the name is also important. In other words, the power of the name works if the person who mentions it represents the name properly in his or her own life. If we Christians live and proclaim the Gospel, God will confirm his word with signs and wonders. Demons will recognise God's presence and leave people. The seven sons of Sceva did not achieve what they wanted because they were not living for Christ. The man who was possessed by evil spirit acknowledged Paul and the work that he was doing.

Strongholds Demolished

Paul's ministry in Ephesus also shows how Christians can destroy the strongholds of Satan. Some of the people who believed the message were former agents of Satan and his demons. These people had been dealing with occult practices. Acts reports:

> The story of what happened spread quickly all through Ephesus, to Jews and Greeks alike. A solemn fear descended on the city, and the name of the Lord Jesus was greatly honored. [18] Many who became believers confessed their sinful practices. [19] A number of them who had been practicing magic brought their incantation books and burned them at a public bonfire. The value of the books was several million dollars. [20] So the message about the Lord spread widely and had a powerful effect (Acts 19.17-20, NLT).

Dealing with magic and using incantations means they were dealing with the occult or demonic. The value of the money, several millions of dollars (cedis), shows that they were making money from the business. Satan had built a stronghold there. The preaching of the Word broke down this stronghold and caused the people to surrender their incantation books.

Notice that Ephesus was a demonic stronghold, yet Paul preached the Word without waging contemporary practices of spiritual warfare. The way believers can help people in any stronghold of the devil is to pray for them and preach the gospel. Without the preaching of the gospel almost nothing will be accomplished. Of course, we have to pray for the people in the territory of such strongholds of Satan. But spending time in spiritual mapping, pulling down territorial spirits will have almost no effect. You may know some issues concerning the city and get prepared for your crusade or evangelistic meetings. However, these activities will not really pull down the territory spirits.

David Servant has a strong and thought-provoking statement which needs to be brought here:

> Christians can scream at principalities and powers all day and night; they can attempt to torment the devil by so-called 'warring tongues'; they can say 'I bind you evil spirits over this city' a million times; they can do all these things up in the airplanes and on the top floors of skyscrapers (as some actually do); and the only way the evil spirits will be affected is that they will get a good laugh at the foolish Christians.[122]

Servant may have gone overboard when he used the term 'foolish' to describe Christians who scream at satanic powers, but I have often made similar statements without using that pejorative word. Nevertheless, Servant's point is valid: if we want to set people free, our efforts need to focus on living like Christ and proclaiming the gospel. The issue is that Satan has deceived people with false thoughts and ideas. The way that people can get freedom from the devil and these false philosophies is to repent and receive the gospel. The proclamation of the Word and the confirmation by God are the real business. Once the gospel is preached, people have the opportunity to believe and accept Jesus. When people believe, they are loosed from the powers of Satan. If people refuse to accept Jesus, God will allow them to remain in darkness. Jesus told his disciples, 'If a village doesn't welcome you or listen to you, shake off the dust of that place from your feet as you leave. I assure you, the

---

[122] Servant, *The Disciple-Making Minister* (Pittsburgh: Ethnos Press, 2005), p. 430. The book is also available online at: www.shepherdserve.org/books/books. htm. Accessed: November 21, 2007.

wicked cities of Sodom and Gomorrah will be better off on the judgment day than that place will be' (Mt. 10.14-15, NLB).

In Ephesus, Paul exposed the secret work of Satan and set people free in Christ by preaching the Word consistently. The Word sets people free and brings them out of darkness. The Word must be preached in season and out of season. This is the greatest charge given to the soldiers of the cross.

22

THE POWER OF TESTIMONY

Another effective weapon against the devil is testimony or witness. This is another facet of the sword of the Spirit. The book of Revelation is very clear about this:

> Then I heard a loud voice shouting across the heavens, 'It has happened at last – the salvation and power and kingdom of our God, and the authority of his Christ! For the Accuser has been thrown down to earth – the one who accused our brothers and sisters before our God day and night. And they have defeated him because of the blood of the Lamb and because of their testimony. And they were not afraid to die' (Rev. 12.10-12, NLT).

Here, John speaks about the defeat of Satan, the Accuser of the brothers and sisters. The defeat was not carried out by praying or preaching but by the blood of the lamb and the testimony of the believers. What is the testimony? How is testimony different from preaching? William Evans defines preaching as 'the proclamation of the Good News of salvation through man to men.'[123] This is to say that in preaching, we present the word of God directly. Testimony is different. In testimony, we witness about what we have seen. Other synonyms for testimony are evidence and proof. Derek Prince gives a very good description of testimony, 'Testimony is speaking from personal experience about incidents that relate to the Word of God and confirm the truth of God's word.'[124] In testimony

---

[123] William Evans, *How to Prepare Sermons* (Chicago: Moody Press, 1964), p. 11.
[124] Derek Prince, *Spiritual Warfare* (Springdale: Whitaker, 1987), p. 129.

we tell people what we have experienced, felt or seen about God and his Word.

In preaching, we bring forth God's principles and promises, but in testimony we show forth by experience what God's promises or principles have done in our lives. For example, if we preach about God's love and forgiveness, we tell people about the principles on which God forgives people. However, if we testify about God's love, we tell people that we have become recipients of God's forgiveness. To give another example, a person may preach about the power of God to heal, without the person experiencing healing before. But the person who testifies about healing has been a beneficiary of healing. Thus, while both preaching and testimony are based upon the Word of God, testimony describes our personal experiences.

Jesus' Strategy to Win the World

The evangelistic wing of The Church of Pentecost is called Witness Movement.[125] The term was derived from Jesus' last command given to his disciples before ascending to heaven. 'But you shall receive power when the Holy Spirit has come upon you; and you shall be witnesses to Me in Jerusalem, and in all Judea and Samaria, and to the end of the earth' (Acts 1.8, NKJV). The Church of Pentecost named the evangelistic wing Witness Movement because it wanted the members to have a personal relationship with Jesus before talking about Him. Witness Movement members were often required to share their personal experiences at Movement meetings before they shared them with outsiders. After such meetings, they were encouraged to share their experiences with others.

Testimonies have been responsible for the planting of many of our churches. The branches that were started outside Ghana were mostly established by members who went abroad for business concerns and began to share their testimonies with others. When new converts were won, these Christians started prayer meetings with

---

[125] The Church of Pentecost was listed as the largest Protestant Christian denomination in Ghana by the last empirical church survey of the Ghana Evangelism Committee. Ghana Evangelism Committee, *National Church Survey: Facing the Unfinished Task of the Church in Ghana* (Accra: Ghana Evangelism Committee, 1993), pp. 16-19.

them and then sent messages to the Church's headquarters in Accra. Representatives were then sent to follow up, and then pastors were sent to shepherd the flock.[126] This shows the power of witnessing.

In Acts 1.8, Jesus said His disciples would be His witnesses. In other words, those who communicate about Jesus would be those who had experienced him. Jesus did not expect people merely to preach about him, but he wanted people who had seen, heard, felt and experienced Him. Being Jesus' witnesses means the responsibility is more than preaching or shouting God's message, but our very lives are to be part of the witnessing. This is why witnessing is so important. People who are witnesses of Jesus do so with emotions and zeal because they communicate with their very lives as well as their words.

Here again, Paul was a very good example of a witness. This is pictured in the Acts of the Apostles:

[4] 'Then he said, 'The God of our fathers has chosen you that you should know His will, and see the Just One, and hear the voice of His mouth. [15] 'For you will be *His witness* to all men of what you have seen and heard. [16] 'And now why are you waiting? Arise and be baptized, and wash away your sins, calling on the name of the Lord.' [17] 'Now it happened, when I returned to Jerusalem and was praying in the temple, that I was in a trance [18] and saw Him saying to me, 'Make haste and get out of Jerusalem quickly, for they will not receive your *testimony* concerning Me' (Acts 22.14-18, emphasis mine).

But the following night the Lord stood by him and said, 'Be of good cheer, Paul; for as you *have testified for Me* in Jerusalem, so you must also *bear witness* at Rome' (Acts 23.11, NJKV, emphasis mine).

[15] 'So I said, 'Who are You, Lord?' And He said, 'I am Jesus, whom you are persecuting. [16] But rise and stand on your feet; for I have appeared to you for this purpose, to make you a minister and *a witness* both of the things which you have seen and of the

---

[126] For an essay on the mission activities of The Church of Pentecost, see Opoku Onyinah, 'Pentecostalism and the African Diaspora: An Examination of the Missions Activities of the Church of Pentecost', *PNEUMA* 26.2 (2004), pp. 216-41.

things which I will yet reveal to you. [17] I will deliver you from the *Jewish* people, as well as *from* the Gentiles, to whom I now send you, [18] to open their eyes, *in order* to turn *them* from darkness to light, and *from* the power of Satan to God, that they may receive forgiveness of sins and an inheritance among those who are sanctified by faith in Me.' (Acts 26.15-18, NKJV, emphasis mine).

In recounting his special encounter with the Lord, Paul emphasised Jesus' commission to testify about what he had seen and heard. Seeing and hearing from the Lord go with power. Once Paul had this encounter and was endued with power, he had the ability to deliver the people from the power of Satan.

Testimony goes with Power

Paul could not minister in his own strength. He had to be filled with the Holy Spirit.

> And Ananias went his way and entered the house; and laying his hands on him he said, 'Brother Saul, the Lord Jesus, who appeared to you on the road as you came, has sent me that you may receive your sight and be filled with the Holy Spirit.' [18]Immediately there fell from his eyes *something* like scales, and he received his sight at once; and he arose and was baptized (Acts 9.17-18, NKJV).

We can only witness about Jesus with His supernatural power. The filling of Paul with the Holy Spirit was what empowered him to break the strongholds of Satan in people.

Jesus assured the disciples, 'You shall receive power when the Holy Spirit has come upon you' (Acts 1.8, NKJV). This means, we need to experience the power of the Holy Spirit before we tell others what Jesus has done for us. The power that accompanies witnessing overcomes the devil.

Now let us return to our original text in Rev. 12.11, '... And they overcame him by the blood of the Lamb and by the word of their testimony, and they did not love their lives to the death' (NKJV). The context reveals that there was war in heaven. The believers were able to overcome the devil. They defeated him with the blood of the Lamb and the word of their testimony. What does this mean?

It means that when believers testify about the Lord Jesus Christ, they experience the power of Jesus' death and resurrection. Through Jesus' death and resurrection he has made the devil powerless. The devil has no control over believers again because of Jesus' death on the cross. The blood symbolises the death. When believers personally testify about Christ, we release his power that deals with the devil and his demonic kingdom. The power is not in mentioning the 'blood of Jesus' but in knowing and understanding what the death of Jesus has meant for humanity and proclaiming this openly. Applying the meaning of Jesus' death is the power that defeats the devil. You always need to remind yourself that the death of Jesus has set humanity free from Satan's hold (Col. 2.13-15). Again, remind yourself that through the blood of Jesus we are forgiven (Eph. 1.7), justified (Rom. 5.9), redeemed (Eph. 1.7), and sanctified (Heb. 13.12). The blood of Jesus continually cleanses believers.[127]

The confession of what Jesus has done for us is the weapon that breaks the power of Satan. Christians will be doing the devil a lot of harm if we positively testify about Jesus in our lives. This calls for personal knowledge of Jesus and what he has done for you as an individual. The declaration of this will release people who are under the bondage of Satan.

---

[127] Review Chapter Five to remind yourself what our Lord Jesus has done for us.

23

PRAYER

After Paul listed the weapons of the Roman soldier as an illustration of the weapons that the Christian needed, he continued with what did not need an illustration. This is prayer:

> Pray at all times and on every occasion in the power of the Holy Spirit. Stay alert and be persistent in your prayers for all Christians everywhere. [19] And pray for me, too. Ask God to give me the right words as I boldly explain God's secret plan that the Good News is for the Gentiles, too. [20] I am in chains now for preaching this message as God's ambassador. But pray that I will keep on speaking boldly for him, as I should (Eph. 6.18-20, NLT).

Paul's intent was that believers would pray at all times and on every occasion. This means prayer is a weapon that must be included in our fight of faith. It must be done always. Other versions, such as New King James and New International lay emphasis on the point that it must be 'all kinds of prayer'. In 1 Timothy 2.1-2, Paul explains further by what he means by 'all kinds of prayer': 'Therefore I exhort first of all that supplications, prayers, intercessions, *and* giving of thanks be made for all men, for kings and all who are in authority, that we may lead a quiet and peaceable life in all godliness and reverence (NKJV)'.

Here we realise that communication with God includes supplications, prayers, intercession, and giving of thanks. Some biblical scholars think that the four words used may be progressive as well as comprehensive. 'Supplications' are for requests for the meeting of needs, 'prayers' are the general conversations with God; 'intercession' is boldly accessing God's presence to make known your requests, and 'thanksgiving' is appreciating God for His mercies and answered prayers.[128] For Mathew Henry 'supplications' are requests for the averting of evil, 'prayers' are for obtaining good, 'intercessions' are requests for others, and 'thanksgivings' are for mercies already received.[129]

What must be said here is that distinguishing one type of prayer from another is not easy, but Paul was trying to teach that prayer can take many forms. He was only giving general headings, but he stressed that prayers must be made for all people. Generally, we should begin by strengthening ourselves in the Lord and making personal requests. Then, prayer must be offered for all people. Worship, praises, and thanksgiving must always be given to God.

Many books have been written about prayers. I shall not like to repeat them. The approach that I adopt here is pragmatic and pastoral. I have put down some of the issues that I often pray on in my personal devotion as a guide for you. Worship, praise, and thanksgiving are dealt with in another chapter; therefore, I have not included them here. All of these are weapons that will help demolish the stronghold of the devil.

In my daily devotions, I read the Bible, worship, and pray on one of the following issues.

Praying for Yourself

Scripture Reading: Ps. 27.1-14; Isa. 62.6-7; Jer. 17.7-18; Heb. 1.8-9

Pray that you Remain in the Lord Forever
Pray for spiritual growth that you will continue to live in Christ, being rooted and built up in him. Pray for a greater desire to pray and read the Word.

Pray to Walk Worthy in the Lord
Ask to stay in purity and holiness, and that you will shun evil. Pray that the Holy Spirit will cause you to follow the Lord faithfully and

---

[128] A.M. Stibbs, 'The Pastoral Epistles', in *The New Bible Commentary Revised* (D. Guthrie, et. al, eds.; Leicester: Inter-Varsity Press, 1970), p. 1171.

[129] Matthew Henry, *Matthew Henry's Commentary on the Bible* (Maclean, VA: MacDonald Publishing Company), VI, p. 811.

that you will desire spiritual things, such as kindness, goodness, patience, longsuffering, and self-control.

Pray to be Filled with the Knowledge of God's will.
Pray for wisdom in making daily decisions. Pray that every action you take will be pleasing to God.

Pray for Increased Physical Strength and Divine Protection
Without good health, no one can do the work of God effectively. With good health people can enjoy life well. Pray for divine health. Pray that the Lord will continue to protect you from Satanic deception and sin.

Pray for Personal Needs
Pray that your service to the Lord will always be acceptable. Pray also that every act of yours will be pleasing to God and for His glory. Ask that you will be content with wherever God places you and that you will remain faithful to him. Pray for any other personal needs.

Pray that the Lord Will Give You His Message
This is important for preachers and leaders. This is praying that you get the right message at the right time.

Pray for Increased Joy
The joy of the Lord is the strength of believers. Fruitfulness needs to be mixed with joy. As a contagious ingredient, joy makes people appreciate your actions. Joy is very important for a leader. If you are a leader, you must pray for joy in service. Spirituality must go with joy. Pray that the Lord will impart joy into your spirit.

Pray for Divine Revelation
Pray that you will be filled with the knowledge of God's will for all of your services to God.

Pray for God's Wisdom
This is necessary for leaders. Pray that the Lord will grant you wisdom to help you know where you are going and how to get there. Then, pray that you will have wisdom to help others know where they are going and how to get there. Ask the Lord to help you apply practically what you know theoretically.

Pray for an Increase of Patience
Ask the Lord to give you the ability to wait patiently when under pressure and stress. Pray that you will have the ability to put up with difficult situations over extended periods.

Pray for a Spirit of Discernment
Pray that the Lord will help you to perceive the nature and significance of problems that arise. Ask the Lord to help you see the problems as He sees them – to know if the causes are physical, spiritual, temperamental, or demonic. Pray that you will know what you ought to do in every situation that develops each day.

Pray for Increased Effectiveness
Ask the Lord to make you more productive and effective in whatever you do. Pray that he will give you lasting fruit from your works. Pray that the Lord will confirm his Word in your life and ministry with signs and miracles.

Pray for Your Personal Responsibilities
If you have been assigned any special duties, such as being a member of a committee or board, pray for the role you play. Pray for your team members. Pray that you will work as a team sharing a similar mission. Ask that there will not be any divisions among you, and that you will be able to forgive one another.

Praying for Church Leadership

The leadership of a church can include many people, such as the Executive Council members, Standing Committee members, Apostles, Prophets, Evangelists, Bishops, Area Heads, Pastors, Overseers, Elders, Deacons, Deaconesses, Movement Leaders, and Committee Leaders.
Scripture Reading: Mt. 9.37-38; Rom. 15.30-33; 1 Cor. 1.8-11; Col. 1.9-14

Pray for Divine Revelation for the Leaders
Pray that the leaders will be filled with the knowledge of God's will for their lives and for their services to God. Pray also that every act of the leaders will be pleasing to God and for His glory.

Pray for God's Wisdom for the Leaders
Pray that the Lord will grant them wisdom to help them know where they are going, and how to get there. Ask the Lord to help them apply practically what they know theoretically.

Pray for an Increase of Patience for the Leaders
Ask the Lord to give them the ability to wait patiently when under pressure and stress. Pray that they will have the ability to put up with difficult situations over extended periods.

Pray for a Spirit of Discernment for the Leaders
Pray that the Lord will help them to perceive the nature and significance of problems that arise. Ask the Lord to help them see whether the roots of the problems are physical, spiritual, temperamental or demonic. Pray that the leaders will know what they ought to do in each situation that develops.

Pray that the Leaders Walk Worthy of God's Call
Pray that the leaders will walk in God's holiness, that they will shun evil deeds and live lives worthy of their calling.

Pray for Increased Effectiveness of the Leaders
Ask the Lord to make the leaders more productive and effective. Pray that he will give them lasting fruit from their works. Pray that the Lord will confirm his word with signs and miracles through the ministry of the leaders.

Pray that the Lord Will Give the Pastors and Other Leaders His Message
Pray that the leaders get the right message at the right time.

Pray for Increased Physical Strength and Protection for Leaders and their Families
Without good health, no one can do the work of God effectively. Road accidents, deaths, illnesses of church leaders seem to be on the increase. Pray that the Lord will intervene. Pray for divine protection for the leaders and their families.

Pray for Increased Joy for the Leaders
The joy of the Lord is the strength of believers. Fruitfulness needs to be mixed with joy. As a contagious ingredient, joy makes others appreciate the leaders' actions. Spirituality must go with joy. Pray that the Lord imparts joy on the leaders.

Praying for the Church

Scripture Reading: Jn 17.20-26; 1 Cor. 12.7-18; Gal. 5.22-26; Eph. 1.15-23; 3.14-21; 4.11-16; Col. 1.9-12; 1 Thess. 3.6-13

Pray for Unity in the Church
Pray that the believers' love will increase and overflow. Pray that there will be unity among all officers, church workers, executives, movement executives, committee members, people in places of service, and all church members.

Pray for the Church Universal
Believers are to love one another and extend that love to those in the world. Pray for cooperation among the church international (the universal church). Pray for all churches including Pentecostal, Charismatic, Evangelical, Catholic, and Indigenous-Initiated Churches. Ask the Lord to reveal himself to churches that have lost the vision (salvation in Christ). Pray that the doctrines of justification by faith, the virgin birth, the death of Christ, and his resurrection will be maintained by all churches.

Pray for God's Holiness in the Church
Ask the Lord that the Church will maintain purity, integrity, and righteousness. Pray for the overcoming of evil desires in the Christians' lives. Ask the Lord to cause Christians to desire the fruit of the Holy Spirit – that is, love, joy, peace, patience, kindness, goodness, faithfulness, gentleness, and self-control.

Pray for the Spiritual Growth of the Church
Pray that believers will continue to live in Christ, being rooted and built up in Him, and strengthened in the faith, just as it is in the Scriptures. Pray that Christians will mature and not behave like infants tossed back and forth by the waves, and blown here and there by every wind of teaching of men. Pray that the Church will not be caught off guard by the cunning and craftiness of men in their deceitful scheming for money and public glorification. Pray that the Church will become mature, attaining to the whole measure of the fullness of Christ. Pray for genuine and sustained revival across churches and nations.

Pray for the Manifestation of Spiritual Gifts in all Churches

Pray that the Lord will bestow spiritual gifts on all Christians. Pray that all those endowed with spiritual gifts will not leave to establish their own ministries and denominations, but will remain and serve in their mother churches. Pray that pride and super-spirituality will not overtake those gifted with power and gifts of revelation. Pray that all the gifts will be used for the building of the Church. Ask the Lord to raise up Apostles, Prophets, Evangelists, Pastors, and Teachers within the churches.

Pray for the Missions Activities of the Church

Pray that the mission activities of the churches will continue to grow. Pray that the Lord will give us the right human, educational, and material resources to promote the Gospel. Pray that the Church will be able to spread the Gospel to all nations and develop the appropriate institutional capacities to contain and manage the growth. Pray also that the Church will effectively integrate the proclamation of the gospel with the appropriate social services and action. Pray that there will breakthroughs in reaching indigenous peoples. Pray that the prophetic mandate of the Church in the world will be pursued and fulfilled.

Praying for Those in Authority and Governments

Scripture Reading: 2 Chron. 33.11-13; Prov. 28.2-5; Dan. 2.20-21; Micah 6.8; 1 Tim. 2.1-4

The task of the Church cannot be carried out effectively when there is no peace in the nations. An atmosphere of peace is the best climate for evangelism. Because of restrictive laws enacted by some heads of state, Christians must make those in authority a primary focus for prayer. This important area of influence includes the following:

The Political Arena

This area includes elected, appointed, or self-imposed officials who are involved in every aspect of government, such as Presidents, Heads of State, Prime Ministers, all political advisors, and religious leaders. Pray that the leaders govern with respect to human rights, and religious and Christian freedom. Pray that all the plans of unjust leaders will fail. Pray that leaders in troubled nations will grow weary of murdering innocent people. Ask God to cause them to recognise that they need help from others to succeed.

The Judicial Arena

This category includes those responsible for interpreting and enforcing the laws that govern the land. These include judges, policemen, military leaders, and all law-enforcement agencies. Pray that they will execute their work with reverent fear for God. Ask God that they will carry out their functions truthfully, honestly, and fairly. Pray that judges will respect Christian values.

The Spiritual Arena

This includes Pastors, Priests, Rabbis, Mallams, and all other religious leaders. Pray that those who do not know Christ will come to know him and accept him as Lord and Saviour. Pray that they will recognise that God alone gave them their positions of authority and that they must walk humbly before Him.

The Educational Arena

This area of influence includes teachers of all levels, from kindergarten to university. Pray that teachers will teach in the fear of God. Pray that unbelievers will not teach their evil ideologies and philosophies. Ask the Lord to cause them to repent and accept Christ.

The Cultural Arena

This area covers all areas of culture such as the arts, sports, music, and entertainment of all types. Entertainment attracts the attention of millions of people throughout the world. Pray for those involved in leading this area. Pray that outmoded cultural practices will end and that sexually induced entertainment will be stopped.

The Media

This includes television, radio, internet, newspapers, as well as influential people in the advertising industry. Pray for key corporate executives and television and radio news personalities to promote Christianity. Pray that Christians will be able to infiltrate the existing television and radio stations. Pray also for the establishment of more Christian television and radio programmes.

The Business or Commercial Arena

This consists of the heads and principal officers of corporations and institutions, such as chief executive officers, managing directors, managers, and accountants. Pray that they will work without partiality in righteousness and in the fear of God. Pray that corrupt business people will realise their evil ways and turn to God. Ask the Lord to cause them to encounter circumstances that will draw them to Him.

The Social Arena
This includes all leaders of influence over any group that may not be mentioned already. It covers leaders over social groups, ethnic groups, clan chiefs, and kings. Pray that they will carry out their functions on a foundation of faithfulness, the fear of God, and righteousness.

Pray for Your Family and Friends
Pray for your spouse (wife or husband), children, father, mother, in-laws, relatives, and friends.

Pray for every member of your family and friends.

Pray for those who have asked for special prayers from you.

Praying for the Salvation of the World

The work of the Church includes the evangelisation of the world. We can accomplish this through preaching the Word and praying for the world.

Scripture Reading: 1 Chron. 16.23-24; Pss. 67.1-3; 86.9-10; 87.1-7; Mt. 28.19-20; Jn 17.20; 1 Tim. 2.1-4; Rev. 5.9-10.

Pray for Everyone in the Nation
This includes praying for every ethnic group (smaller linguistic groups within a nation), every tongue (languages and dialects), and every people (human beings and individuals of a particular race). Pray that people called of God will offer themselves for evangelism. Pray for all workers in this area, such as the evangelists, missionaries, Bible societies, and evangelism societies.

Pray Against Satanic Strongholds in the Nations
Pray against governmental strongholds. This includes praying against satanic laws like legalized abortion, tolerance of homosexuality, promotion of atheism, and laws restricting the preaching of the Gospel.

Pray Against Occultism
Pray against the growth of occultism such as divination, spiritism, witchcraft, sorcery, and astral projection

Pray Against Cultural Strongholds
Pray against evil elements in the culture that hinder the promotion and growth of the Gospel. Pray also that the Church will have wisdom in dealing with cultural practices such as the yearly banning of drumming in Accra, chieftaincy, the pouring of libations, the offerings of sacrifice to the gods, and the forbidding of farm work on special days.

Pray Against Religious Strongholds
Some world religions are Islam, Buddhism, and Hinduism. Newer religions include Jehovah's Witnesses, Mormonism, and the New Age Movement. Pray against satanic beliefs that enslave entire nations or major people groups of a nation.

Pray Against Materialistic Strongholds
Materialism has become a major stronghold that hinders some people from accepting the Gospel and sacrificing for it. Pray against satanic desires and the continuous lust for wealth.

Pray for all Evangelistic Activities of the Church
Prayer should be made for various evangelistic activities of the Church. This includes open-air services, crusades, rallies, street evangelism, door-to-door evangelism, literature evangelism, personal evangelism, and radio and TV evangelism.

Pray for the Lost
Pray that the lost will begin to ask themselves about whom they are trusting, and they will begin to search for Christ. Pray that God will cause them to question the lies they hear from their political, religious, social leaders – and from their friends.

Ask the Holy Spirit to haunt them with the question, 'What is my purpose for living?' As they see all things to be useless and vain their attention may be drawn to Christ. Pray that the lost will begin to ask themselves how they can cope with their problems. It seems every individual in the world faces some problems beyond his or her capabilities. Ask the Holy Spirit to plant a sense of the hopelessness of sin in their hearts. This will cause the lost to realise their need for help and also prepare their hearts for the Gospel. Pray that

God will cause unbelievers to ponder over where they will go when they die. This will eventually turn into a quest for eternal life. The Gospel will then become the only tangible solution.

Pray for the Salvation of your Loved Ones
This includes praying for your spouse if he or she is not a Christian, your children, your parents, your relatives, and your friends.

Pray for the Sick
Pray for the sick and afflicted. This includes all those who are weak, feeble, or sick and those who are oppressed mentally, physically, socially, or spiritually. Pray that through their afflictions those who do not know Christ will accept Him into their lives. Pray that through their afflictions those who know Him will love Him more.

Pray against the HIV and AIDS epidemic and ask God to reveal cures for incurable diseases.

I believe this is an important part of breaking the stronghold of the devil. If Christians will do the business of prayer, a lot will be accomplished for Christ. However, talking about prayer and praying are two different things. I encourage you to pray. When you do, you will receive strength for your Christian life, and you will serve the Lord faithfully without fearing the devil and his power.

24

THE ROLE OF DELIVERANCE IN WARFARE

Many Christians want to know more about the role of deliverance in spiritual warfare. We have learned that there is power in the word of God, that it always accomplishes its purpose. Salvation is real. If God says he has saved a person from the kingdom of darkness, it is true because God does not lie. However, what about Christians who come from occult backgrounds, or believers who struggle with on-going sin, chronic illnesses, or persistent financial problems? Although I have indirectly addressed those concerns already, here I offer some pastoral guidance to ministers who offer 'deliverance' to such people.

To begin with, let me offer some definitions. 'Demon possession' – though not a biblical term – is often used to mean that there are some Satanic evil spirits who take control of people, use them, and seek their destruction. 'Exorcism' usually means casting out a demon from a person who is possessed. 'Deliverance' is usually distinguished from exorcism and means freeing people from the influence or bondage of Satan and demons who are behind afflictions, sufferings, bad habits, curses, and failures in life. However, in this chapter deliverance includes exorcism, and I will also introduce a new term, 'witchdemonology.'[130]

---

[130] The term has actually been introduced at Chapter 10. The term describes the beliefs and practices of 'deliverance ministries' in Africa, which is a synthesis of the practices and beliefs of African witchcraft and Western Christian demonology and exorcism.

Demonic Influence and Christians

Many evangelical Christians agree with the practice of casting out demons from non-Christians. However, there is much disagreement about the contemporary practice of deliverance of Christians. I shall like to briefly discuss this issue from a biblical perspective before offering pastoral counselling.

The Old Testament indicates that evil spirits may influence the lives of disobedient people of God. For example, 1 Samuel records that Saul was filled with the Holy Spirit and prophesied (1 Sam. 10.6, 10). But later, the Spirit of God departed from him and on some occasions 'an evil spirit from the Lord tormented him' (1 Sam. 16.14, 23; 1 Sam. 18.10-11; 1 Sam. 19.9-10).

The suffering of Saul has been considered from different angles; for example, it is considered psychologically as 'depression' or 'mental illness'.[131] However, the text is clear that Saul was indeed troubled by an evil spirit,[132] and David's playing of the harp was one means of 'exorcising' the spirit (1 Sam. 16.14-23). Hertzberg says this was a genuine exorcism and music has been 'a means elsewhere in such situations'.[133] In other words, David's type of 'exorcism' can be related to contemporary deliverance. A 'witchdemonologist' or a deliverance minister would say that Saul's case was very probably an Old Testament example of a believer being 'demonised' or experiencing 'demonisation' – and, as such, needed deliverance.[134]

The detailed accounts of Jesus' confrontation with demoniacs[135] and several summaries of his ministry indicate that exorcism was an integral part of his work and that demonic influence was common

---

[131] See John Mauchline, *1 and 2 Samuel: New Century Bible* (London: Oliphants, 1971), pp. 130-31; Hans Wilhelm Hertzberg, *1 & 11 Samuel: Old Testament Library*, 2nd ed. (trans. J. S. Bowden; London: SCM Press Ltd, 1972), pp. 140-41.

[132] Samuel had regarded the sin of disobedience as witchcraft (1 Sam. 15.23).

[133] Hertzberg, *1 & 11 Samuel*, p. 141.

[134] Some Christians say that since this took place before Pentecost, such situations are not possible in this age. However, for other views, please see: C. Fred Dickason, *Demon Possession and the Christian* (Chicago: Moody Press, 1987), pp. 123, 127-38; Merrill F. Unger, *What Demons Can Do to Saints* (Chicago: Moody Press, 1977), pp. 51-52.

[135] The four main narratives of Jesus' exorcisms are Mk 1.21-28; cf. Lk. 4.31-37; Mt. 8.28-34; cf. Mk 5.1-17; cf. Lk. 8.26-37; Mt. 15.21-28; cf. Mk 7.24-30; Mk 9.14-29; cf. Mt. 17.14-19; cf. Lk. 9.37-45).

in Jesus' time.[136] The accounts of the demoniac in the Capernaum synagogue (Mk 1.21-28; cf. Lk. 4.31-37) indicates that the demoniac was somebody who was well settled and involved in the life of the community; in our time, he would be a churchgoer. Yet, this man was inhabited by demons. Though this was before Pentecost, it tells us that demons can influence people of that calibre.

Some passages in the gospel of John say that Judas, the apostle of Jesus, was 'possessed by the devil'. For example, John records that the devil puts the thought of betrayal 'into the heart of Judas' (Jn 13.2, KJV). Later, 'Satan entered into him' (Jn 13.27, KJV).[137] The issue of Judas is important because he was an apostle of Jesus Christ. But was he actually possessed? The text indicates that Satan entered into his heart. Satan could not enter him physically, this implies Satan invisibly entered into him and influenced him to act the way he did. Thus the idea of possession was in the background. The idea of possession was widespread among Jews and Gentiles.[138] Although this incident took place before Pentecost, deliverance teachers may see in this story the possibility of a Christian being possessed by demons.

Another case that needs consideration is the filling of the heart of Ananias with lies by Satan. Peter speaks to Ananias, 'How is it that Satan has so filled your heart that you have lied against the Holy Spirit?' (Acts 5.3, NIV). Ananias was a believer, yet the devil was able to fill his heart with evil. Barrett rightly argues that the telling

---

[136] These include brief reports of exorcisms by Jesus (Mt. 9.32-34; 12.22), a brief report of the disciples' mission (Lk. 10.17), a number of references and sayings on Jesus' dealings with demons (Mk 1.32-34, 39; 3.7-12) and the accusation of Jesus as demon possessed (Mt. 12.22-28; cf. Mk 3.23-27; cf. Lk. 11.17-22).

The accounts are quite varied, as also in 'witchdemonology.' For example, Jesus approached the demoniacs in some of the narratives (Lk. 8.26-39; 11.14). In others, the demons manifested themselves (Mk 1.21-28; cf. Lk. 4.31-37). In another case, He recognized Satan in a debilitating illnesses (Lk. 13.11-16). At other times, Jesus responded to requests from a parent or friends (Mk 9.14-29; cf. Lk. 9.37-43; Mt. 12.22). See Robert A. Guelich, 'Spiritual Warfare: Jesus, Paul and Peretti', *PNEUMA* 13.1 (1991), pp. 39-41.

[137] Here the Authorised Version and the New American Standard Version both follow the literal translation of the Greek. See Alfred Marshall, *The NASB Interlinear Greek English New Testament* (Grand Rapids: Regency, 1984), p. 423.

[138] Rudolf Bultmann, *The Gospel of John: A Commentary* (trans. G. R. Beasley-Murray, gen. ed.; Philadelphia: Westminster Press, 1971), p. 482.

of the lie 'expresses the result of Satan's filling Ananias heart'.[139]
There is no indication here of Satanic possession, though Satan certainly influenced Ananias to tell a lie so that he could keep some of
his money from the sale of the land.

The epistles do not directly mention the demonisation of Christians; however, numerous passages (2 Cor. 11.2-4, 13-15; 1 Tim.
3.6-7; 4.1; 2 Tim. 2.25-26; 2 Pet. 2.1-22) warn that Christians stand
in real danger of being tempted, falling, and being controlled by
demons, if they are not careful to remain completely in the faith.[140]
Some Christian ministers (and scholars) also see 'demonisation'
of Christians in Eph. 4.27, which reads, 'And do not give the devil a
foothold' (NIV).[141] Dwelling upon the translation of the Greek
word *topos* as inhabiting place, Clinton Arnold proposes that Eph.
4.27 is the 'closest [Paul] came to the 'possession language' in the
New Testament.[142] This text is insufficient as a basis for demonisation of Christians because the verse does not go that far. Lincoln,
for example, contends that 'the writer thinks in terms of a personal
power of evil, which is pictured as lurking around angry people
ready to exploit the situation'.[143] Accordingly, the verse may best be
considered a representation of several passages in the epistles that
speak of the devil taking advantage of Christians as the result of sin
in their lives (2 Cor. 2.11; 11.3; Jas 4.7; 1 Pet. 5.8). What is clear
from these passages is that Paul and other New Testament writers
deal with the reality of evil and of human beings enslaved by pow-

---

[139] C.K. Barrett, *Acts: The International Critical Commentary* (J.A. Emerson,
C.E.B. Cranfield and G.N. Stanton, eds. Latest Impression; Edinburgh: T & T
Clark, 1998), p. 266.

[140] For further study of demon possession and Christians see David Powlison,
Power Encounters: Reclaiming Spiritual Warfare (Grand Rapid: Baker Books, 1995),
pp. 27-38, 121-36; Clinton A. Arnold, *Spirit Warfare: What Does the Bible Teach?*
(London: Marshall Pickering, 1999), pp. 73-160; Charles H. Kraft, *Defeating the
Dark Angels* (Kent: Sovereign World, 1993), pp. 61-78.

[141] For example, see Ed Murphy, *The Handbook for Spiritual Warfare* Revised
and Updated Edition (Nashville: Thomas Nelson Publishers, 1996), p. 432; Vito
Rallo, *Breaking Generational Curses & Pulling Down Strongholds* (Lake Mary: Creation
House Press, 2000), pp. 1-2; C. Fred Dickason, *Demon Possession and the Christian*
(Chicago: Moody Press, 1987), pp. 107-108.

[142] Clinton E. Arnold, *Powers of Darkness: Principalities and Powers in Paul's Letters*
(Downers Grover: InterVarsity Press, 1992), p. 128.

[143] Andrew T. Lincoln, *Ephesians* (Word Biblical Commentary, vol. 42; Bruce
Metzger, gen. ed.; Nashville: Thomas Nelson, 1990), p. 303.

ers hostile to God. That enslavement is often what some see as 'demonisation'.

The previous Bible passages picture the devil invading the lives of believers, and deliverance ministers use them to support the notion that Christians can be possessed. However, there are no clear indications that the passages support actual demon possession.

Can Christians Be 'Possessed'?

Though the word 'possessed' is in some of our English translations, the word is actually not in the Greek. The Greek words actually refer to people 'having a demon' or 'suffering demonic influence'. Perhaps the Gerasene demoniac was the only example of a person who was completely under Satan's dominion. So can a Christian be possessed? The answer is no because a Christian's will cannot be under Satan's control and Christ's control at the same time. Can a Christian be under Satanic influence? Yes, and 'in all cases, the remedy will be the same anyway: rebuke the demon in the name of Jesus and command it to leave'.[144]

When Deliverance May Not Be Necessary

The role of deliverance should be seen as one means of dealing with a variety of manifestations of evil in human life. In the Gospels, while Jesus sometimes cast out demons, He didn't always do that when he encountered people wrapped up in evil.

The first example is the woman who was caught in adultery (Jn 8.1-11). The issue was very serious because the woman was caught red-handed in the very act. In the Old Testament such a person should have been stoned. Notice that Jesus did not cast out a 'demon of lust' from this woman. His remedy was simple: 'Go and sin no more'. What this woman needed was repentance and right living. She needed to be obedient to the word of God. I often wonder how many 'deliverance ministers' would have forced her through a period of deliverance.

---

[144] Wayne Grudem, *Systematic Theology* (Grand Rapids: Zondervan, 1994), pp. 423-25.

Another case that comes to mind is the woman who 'had lived a sinful life' (Lk. 7.36-47). This woman, who had lived a publicly immoral life, came to Jesus while he was eating dinner, anointed his feet with her tears and her perfume, and dried his feet with her hair. The Pharisee with whom Jesus was eating was not only offended but thought that if Jesus were a prophet, He would never have allowed such a display from a woman of disgrace. Jesus told a story to explain his tolerance and summarised his point to the Pharisee: 'I tell you, her sins – and they are many – have been forgiven, so she has shown me much love. But a person who is forgiven little shows only little love'. Then Jesus said to the woman, 'Your sins are forgiven ... Your faith has saved you; go in peace' (Lk. 7.47-50). Here the remedy for the sinner was forgiveness.

Next, Jesus did not expel a 'demon of lies' from Peter, who betrayed him three times (Lk. 22.31, 22.54-60). Peter was an apostle of Jesus, but he lied three times. When Jesus rose from the dead and asked Peter whether he loved him, he never even referred to Peter's denials. The reason was that he had been forgiven; it was an issue of the flesh and not demonic.

Similarly, when Paul encountered evil, he did not always hunt to chop off Satan's head.

One obvious situation was the man who was having an immoral relationship with his father's wife. Paul did not advise that a 'demon of lust' be cast out of the man. Rather he disciplined him (1 Cor. 5.1-5). Delivering the man to Satan was after the sin and not the cause of it. Again he did not cast out a 'demon of division' from the saints in Corinth, who were divided among personalities (1 Cor. 3.1-9). Furthermore, he did not cast a 'demon of slavery' from the Galatians who had been bewitched (Gal. 3.1-6).[145]

Let's also look at some examples of Old Testament saints who fell into sin. In fact some of the sins were very serious. These include Abraham, who slept with his maid (Gen. 16.1-15); David, who slept with Uriah's wife (2 Sam. 11.1-27); Solomon, who was polygamous and idolatrous (1 Kgs 11.1-8); and Absalom who rebelled against his father (2 Sam. 15.1-12). None of these people were considered demonised.

---

[145] Leon-Joseph Suenens, *Renewal and the Powers of Darkness* (Darton: Longman Todd and Servant Publications, 1983), p. 17.

The point that I am driving at is that deliverance may not be the solution to relentless problems. Other areas need to be considered. Continuous exorcisms may only worsen the situation. In the biblical examples I cited, pastoral care and teaching were the proper medicine.

A counselling session I had with one Akosua will highlight the importance of giving pastoral care to people who feel hopeless and useless.[146] Having been brought up in a religious home, Akosua fell into immorality with a young man she was preparing to marry. Unfortunately, the young man met another girl, broke the relationship – and Akosua's heart. Then, following the break-up, Akosua was raped.

After the rape, she began having very disturbing dreams of being sexually abused by frightening beings. Such dreams had a physical and emotional impact upon her. As a result of these on-going experiences, Akosua felt she could die any moment. She went to different churches and prayer camps for exorcisms under 'great men and women of God', and she prayed and fasted for days and weeks – all to no avail. She did not know whether or not she was a witch or a normal human being.

Akosua felt very insecure as she was telling her story to my assistant and me. She was confused and unsure of herself and future. But her problem was one of the most common problems facing young women in Pentecostal/Charismatic circles. Being trained in a Christian home with a perfectionist attitude but a passionate nature, Akosua believed she had an irreconcilable conflict between sexuality and Christian ethics.

The interpretation that came out of the dreams was that of 'a vulnerable woman' being sexually dominated, deceived, and forced by a male's strength to engage in immorality. Her former boyfriend had repeatedly forced upon her. Although she felt her behaviour was not right, she had been introduced to sexual activity, enjoyed it, but then she was ultimately rejected. As a woman in an African society, she could not force herself on anybody; all she could do was suppress her desires. Yet the suppression was resulting in compulsive behaviours. This may be termed as obsessive-compulsive disorder. This is a condition in which a person experi-

---

[146] Not her real name.

ences recurrent, intrusive thoughts and feels repeatedly compelled to perform certain behaviours and then has flashbacks of previous traumatic events. The images that Akosua saw clearly illustrated her passionate sexuality. The figures, who were always ready to satisfy her sexual needs, perhaps hinted at her wish for power, authority, and the satisfaction of all her preferences.

As long as Akosua felt rejected and that her desires were socially and biblically unacceptable, her deliverance or healing were far off. In fact, in her situation the fasting, the praying, the demand for righteous thinking, the accusations of witchcraft, and the unsuccessful exorcisms only worsened her condition. The problem wasn't with the Gospel but with how it was being applied. What Akosua really needed was genuine pastoral counselling. She needed a caring group of people who would meet with her on a regular basis to help her deal with her rejection, assure her of God's love in the midst of her situation, help her to understand and appropriate Scripture, and hold her accountable for overcoming the problem of lust truly rather than satisfying it demonically.

I assured Akosua of God's love and that God had not rejected her because of her condition. I explained that the desire for a sexual relationship was common to all normal people. Then I assured her that she was a normal human being – not a witch – and that what was happening to her was unique. At this stage, she breathed a sigh of relief and beams of smiles began to radiate from her face. I then explained that God willed for her to be free of lust and that He could set her free – but only with her cooperation. I asked her if I could explain the matter to her Pastor, who would either counsel her or delegate the responsibility to one of the elders. She agreed that I should inform her pastor about it. The Scriptures I read with her before praying included Jn 6.37 and Rom. 5.6-11.[147]

When Deliverance May Be Needed

Deliverance and exorcisms should not be ignored, but let me establish four parameters.

---

[147] See Opoku Onyinah 'Healing and Reconciliation from an African Pentecostal Perspective' in *Healing and Reconciliation: Pastoral Counseling Across Christian Traditions Cultures* (CWME: Athens, 2005), pp. 35-45.

First is theological and this is where the discussion of 'witchde-monology' enters. My experience – and the focus of my doctoral research – has shown me that deliverance in contemporary Africa is based on the persistent belief in witchcraft and other spirit forces and that has resulted in 'witchdemonology'. Again, this is the min-gling of both African traditional religion and Christianity. Important aspects of this theology are the attempts to identify and exorcise demonic forces in people' lives (whether in an individual's life or at a corporate level) in order for them to succeed in the contemporary world. On the positive side, these deliverance ministries are in step with the culture and deal with people's beliefs and fears. Negatively, however, these ministries are much alarming. Their preoccupation with demons and witches shows that it is an affirmation of the old order. They appear to have fallen into the weaknesses of the anti-witchcraft shrines and some of the African Independent Churches. The approach may fit well into the African cultural milieu, but the emphasis is a threat to the progress of Christianity and modernity in Africa. In spite of the rapid growth of these deliverance ministries, their approach cannot bring the African out of the fear of witch-craft and other supernatural powers. I'm not saying we should sup-press these ministries; rather, we must bring them into theological balance.

Second, Jesus gave his followers authority to cast out demons. So, exorcism need not be left to a special group of people who are thought to have special powers. Instead, because Jesus gave His au-thority to all of his followers, exorcism should be opened to the entire prophetic community, but they should be trained to handle this important ministry with proper balance.

Third, Jesus and Paul dealt with demonic situations as they arose. They didn't chase after demons and neither should we. A corollary is that there is no need to set aside a special time or place for acts of deliverance. We must be ready to allow the Holy Spirit to exorcise, deliver, or heal at any time, even during a Sunday service, which is the high point of the Christian week.

Fourth, before engaging in exorcism, be sure that the problem is demonic. If the situation is unclear, counsellors should try other approaches first. If the situation is too complex, the client should be referred to other leaders of the church. Here, prayers of deliverance can be said for the person.

Concluding that a person's case is demonic needs extra care. From his analysis of Jesus' exorcisms, Twelftree identifies the following signs of demonic presence: extraordinary strength, indifference to the pain of the sufferer, vocalisation of distress when confronted by Jesus, and a change in the sufferer's voice.[148] Nevertheless, contemporary Christian psychiatrists show that these symptoms can almost all be explained in some naturalistic way.[149] While this does not rule out the possibility of demonic presence, it shows that many cases which people consider demonic may be natural issues. Therefore, concluding on a demonic activity or witchcraft possession should not be made hastily. If the counsellor has not received discernment or a clear prophetic insight, which must have been accepted by the client, he/she must explore all possible natural explanations.[150]

---

[148] Graham Twelftree, *Christ Triumphant: Exorcism Then and Now* (London: Hodder & Stoughton, 1985), p. 70. Twelftree, 'The Place of Exorcism in Contemporary Ministry', *St Mark's Review* 127 (1986), pp. 25-39. See also John Richards who tries to show a distinction between a possession state and others. John Richards, *But Deliver Us from Evil: An Introduction to the Demonic Dimension in Pastoral Care* (London: Darton, 1974), pp. 91-118, 156-59; John Richards, *Exorcism Deliverance and Healing: Some Pastoral and Liturgical Guidelines* Third Edition (Nottingham: Grove Books Limited, 1990), pp. 12-13.

[149] See Gary R. Collins, 'Psychological Observation on Demonism' and John White 'Commentary on Psychological Observation in Demonism' in John Warwick Montgomery (ed.), *Demon Possession* (Minneapolis: Bethany House Publishers, 1976), pp. 237-245 and 253; David Brewer, 'Jesus and the Psychiatrists', in Anthony N.S. Lane (ed.), *The Unseen World: Christian Reflections on Angels, Demons and the Heavenly Realms* (Carlisle: Paternoster Press, 1996), pp. 133-48; Myrtle S. Langley, 'Spirit-Possession and Exorcism and Social Context: An Anthropological Perspective with Theological Implications', *Churchman* 94.3 (1980), pp. 226-45.

[150] The issue of discernment is controversial. For the gift of discernment of spirits, see Wayne Grudem, *The Gift of Prophecy in 1 Corinthians* (Washington: University Press of America, 1982), pp. 58-74; Grudem, *The Gift of Prophecy in the New Testament Today* (Eastbourne: Kingsway Publications, 1998), pp. 70-72; Gordon Fee, *God's Empowering Presence: The Holy Spirit in the Letters of Paul* (Peabody: Hendrickson, 1994), pp. 171-72; Ralph P. Martin, *The Spirit and the Congregation: Studies in 1 Corinthians 12-15* (Grand Rapids, 1984), pp. 14-15; Arnold Bittlinger, *Gifts and Graces: A Commentary on 1 Corinthians 12-14* (Grand Rapids: Eerdmans, 1967), pp. 45-46. For discerning of spirits, see Amos Yong, *Discerning the Spirit(s): A Pentecostal-Charismatic Contribution to Christian Theology of Religions* (JPTSup 20; Sheffield: Sheffield Academic Press, 2000), pp. 256-309; Timothy J. Gorringe, *Discerning of Spirits: A Theology of Revelation* (London: SCM, 1990). Stephen E. Parker, *Led by the Spirit: Toward a Practical Theology of Pentecostal Discernment and Decision Making* (JPTSup 7; Sheffield: Sheffield Academic Press, 1996), pp. 175-205.

Methods or Techniques of Deliverance Prayer

As to the techniques or methods of deliverance, preferably those used by Jesus are to be followed. Jesus' main method of exorcism was a simple word of command. Jesus did not use any mechanical devices; he often used the simple word of command, either to cast out demons or to heal (Mk 1.25; Lk. 4.35; Mk 5.8; Lk. 8.29; Mt. 8.32; Mk 9.25; Mt. 17.18; Lk. 9.42). On one occasion he commanded a demon not to return to the person (Mk 9.25, cf. Mt. 12.43-45; Lk. 11.24-26). On another occasion, he attempted to know the demon's name (Mk 5.7-8; Lk. 8.28-29). Even here the whole scenario shows that Jesus was in control. The demons did not have any power; they surrendered to the authority of Jesus.

Comparing Jesus' method with the ritualistic techniques used by some deliverance ministers, some areas need to be reconsidered. John White has objected to the use of rituals in exorcisms, since, for him, such an approach is to depend upon magic and undermines dependence on God.[151] But Arnold observes that 'magical beliefs and practices can be found in the mystery religions and even in Judaism and Christianity'.[152] Drawing from David Aune's definition of magic,[153] however, Arnold shows some distinction between religion and magic: 'In religion one prays requests from the gods; in magic one commands the gods and therefore expects guaranteed result.'[154]

---

[151] John White, 'Problems and Procedures in Exorcism', in John Warwick Montgomery (ed.), *Demon Possession*, (Minneapolis: Bethany House Publishers, 1976), pp. 281-99.

[152] Clinton E. Arnold, *Ephesians: Power and Magic. The Concept of Power in Ephesians in Light of Its Historical Setting* (Cambridge: Cambridge University Press, 1989), p. 18. For monotheists, such as Christians and Jews, he contends that 'reliance on the aid of "powers" betrays a lack of confidence in the one God' (p. 18).

[153] Aune gives a two-stage definition of magic. First, he defines magic as 'the form of religious deviance in which individual or social goals are sought by means not normally sanctioned by dominant religious institutions'. He continues that 'second, such religious deviance is magical only when the goals sought within the context of religious deviance are magical when attained through the management of supernatural power in such a way that the results are virtually guaranteed'. David E. Aune, 'Magic, Magician', in Geoffrey Bromiley (ed.), *The International Standard Bible Encyclopedia*, (Grand Rapids: William B. Eerdmans Publishing Co., 1986), p. 214. Note, the second stage is what is important to Arnold. The first part, however, shows that it is a dominant religion that sees some practices of others as magical. In other words, these are not considered magical by those who practise it.

[154] Arnold, *Ephesians: Power and Magic*, p. 18.

Thus 'magical practices' or rituals may not necessarily be magic if the rituals are seen as making a request to the gods. Magico-religious practices have been prominent in Old Testament and Christian traditional practices. These include the rituals in the Old Testaments such as the use of Urim and Thummim and the use of oil in the New Testament (Jas 5.14). Using them may be ways of communicating the biblical message to people. However, the intent is undermined if the practices go against Scripture and the ethical code of the people you are attempting to reach.

In light of this discussion, the preparing of a 'deliverance atmosphere' through worship, drumming, clapping, and long prayers by deliverance ministers can be accommodated, since this helps them carry out their task, and the practices don't cause any harm. Moreover, referring to prayer as the 'fire of God' or the 'axe of God' can be tolerable because although they show a sense of inadequacy on the part of ministers or the people who are praying, the terms do not necessarily cause any harm.

Allowing the 'demons to speak' or the client to project himself/herself outwardly by speaking during deliverance may be accommodated because it can be a way of voicing the real problem. Such speech may help the counsellor or the exorcist understand the real situation and follow up after the exercise. Following up on those things should be the main reason for allowing such utterances because often the things spoken are clues about the main problem. However, this should be done privately and not publicly because the utterance may cause further problems.

Nonetheless, some deliverance practices may be dangerous. These include extracting public confessions from self-claimed witches or demon-possessed victims in order to arrest attention before exorcism. The reason is that naïve people may be responsive to suggestive stories and may assume themselves to be possessed when they actually are not. Also, such confessions can put a social stigma on self-claimed witches and they may never be accepted in society again. Confessions should be made privately, and confession can also be a means of healing or deliverance.

Furthermore, chaining of witches is inhumane, not to mention illegal, while enforcing long periods of fasting and prayer on clients are quite physically dangerous practices as well. Such actions suggest that the ministers have no control over the situations and can obscure the fact that the manifestations exhibited by the individual may be natural and a sign of the need for immediate medical attention. Deliverance ministers sometimes base these latter practices on Jesus' remark that some demons can only come out through prayer and fasting.[155] But that injunction is for the ministers, not the demoniacs.[156] Still again, publicity either before or after deliverance, such as writing down clients' information and announcing them publicly or recording the process of deliverance for sale should be discouraged because they undermine trust and may give the impression that the ministers are using their ministries for money.

Generally, the methods should be simple to show trust in the power of Jesus, whose death has given the believer the authority to exercise this ministry. Too much ritual may reveal a lack of spiritual power on the part of the ministers and a lack of trust in Jesus. The focus should always be on Christ and what he has done for the world. The focus of ministers must be on the Word of God, which will set people free; otherwise Christians will remain babes who will always need the attention of their parents. It is high time ministers help believers to be mature in Christ. This is often demonstrated in our worship, which is our focus, next.

---

[155] Mark 9.29 and Mt. 17.21 in some versions such as the Authorised Version.

[156] Larry W. Hurtado, *Gospel of Mark* (NIBC; Carlisle: Paternoster, 1995), p. 148; William Lane, *The Gospel According to Mark* (NICNT; Grand Rapids: Eerdmans, 1974), pp. 335-36; W.D. Davies and Dale C. Allison Jr., *Critical and Exegetical Commentary on the Gospel According to St. Matthew VIII-XVIII* (London: Continuum Publishing Group, 2004), pp. 726-27; Robert H. Gundry, *Matthew: A Commentary on His Handbook for a Mixed Church Under Persecution*, 2nd ed. (Grand Rapids: Eerdmans, 1994), pp. 352-53.

25

PRAISE AND WORSHIP

There is power in praise and worship. Although Ephesians 6 does not list praise and worship as one of the weapons, it is implicit in verse 18: 'And pray in the Spirit on all occasions with all kinds of prayers and requests.' Praying in the Spirit on all occasions is a life of worship and will bring instability to the devil and his kingdom.

In our contemporary Christian culture, Christians sometimes define praise and worship as the time of singing in church. But biblical worship is more than singing; biblical worship is offering our entire life to God. 'Offer your bodies as living sacrifices, holy and pleasing to God – this is your spiritual act of worship' (Rom. 12.1). Biblical worship is a way of life, not just a song.

The Hebrew term for worship is *shachah,* which means 'to bow down in reverence, worship', or 'to bow down … as a gesture of respect or submission'.[157] To worship is to ascribe ultimate value to a person, an object, or a deity. Reverence, adoration, and homage are paid to the subject of worship. We order the priorities of our lives around that which we worship. For example, some people like sports and ascribe value to certain players to the point that when those superstars are playing, they will pay any amount and travel any distance to watch the game. The way such people put value on athletes and attend to them may be termed as worshipping them. To worship God is to place absolute value on God and honour him that way.

---

[157] Clines, David J. A. (ed.), *The Concise Dictionary of Classical Hebrew* (Sheffield, UK: Sheffield Phoenix Press, 2009), p. 455.

One of the Hebrew terms translated in the Bible as praise is *halal*. The literal meaning of *halal* is to 'shine'.[158] At the heart of this Hebrew root is the idea of radiance. From this came the excitement of rejoicing and praising God. The well-known imperative is *Hallelujah*, which calls for giving the glory to God. To praise a person is to acknowledge in words who the person is. You will need to know the nature and deeds of the person in order to laud the person. For example, you can praise a king or a leader if you know that he is a good person, and more so if he has demonstrated it in many ways to your satisfaction and delight. To praise a person is to tell the person verbally who he is and what he has done. To praise God is to thank him for who he is and what he has done. In praise, your inward attitude explodes in outward expression. In praising God, you help yourself to accept and renew your knowledge of the person of God and what He has done and will continue to do for you.

The Bible does not systematically separate praise from worship or thanksgiving from worship. They are all mixed together. Praise is an aspect of worship.

God Created Us for His Pleasure

When God called the people of Israel, he wanted them to worship him. 'The leaders of the people of Israel will accept your message. Then all of you must go straight to the king of Egypt and tell him, "The LORD, the God of the Hebrews, has met with us. Let us go on a three-day journey into the wilderness to offer sacrifices to the LORD our God" (Exod. 3.18, NLT). This was the instruction that the Lord gave to Moses. The people were to go to the wilderness to offer sacrifice to the Lord. However, in Exod. 7.16, when the Lord was repeating what he said to Moses, He changed 'to offer sacrifices' to 'to worship'. 'Say to him, "The LORD, the God of the Hebrews, has sent me to say, 'Let my people go, so they can worship me in the wilderness. Until now, you have refused to listen to him'"' (Exod. 7.16, NLT). This means the offering of sacrifice amounted to worship. Again, it implies that all the instructions given to the

---

[158] Brown, Francis *et al.*, *The New Brown, Driver, Briggs, Gesenius Hebrew and English Lexicon: With an Appendix Containing the Biblical Aramaic* (trans. Edward Robinson; Peabody, MA: Hendrickson, 1979), p. 237.

people of Israel on sacrifice were toward the worship of God. The purpose of God calling the people of Israel was to worship him.

God delights in worship. Psalm 22.3 declares, 'But thou *art* holy, O *thou* that inhabitest the praises of Israel' (KJV). This means God reveals His glory when we give Him the worship He deserves. In Revelation we are informed of what goes on in heaven: the four living creatures and the twenty-four elders worship God day and night. Part of what they say is, 'You are worthy, O Lord our God, to receive glory and honor and power. For you created everything, and it is for your pleasure that they exist and were created (Rev. 4.11, NLT). This means that God created us for His pleasure. When we sincerely worship God with our entire lives, he receives pleasure. Paul explains this concept in Ephesians, 'Because of his love, God had already decided to make us his own children through Jesus Christ. That was what he wanted and what pleased him, and it brings praise to God because of his wonderful grace. God gave that grace to us freely, in Christ, the One he loves' (Eph. 1.5-6; cf. 1.14 NLT).

Worship Must Be in Holiness

Although God takes pleasure in our worship, he does not want us to worship him in dirt. Because God is holy, his people must worship him in holiness. The Lord instructs, 'After all, I, the LORD, am your God. You must be holy because I am holy' (Lev. 11.44a, NLT). Therefore, in the Old Covenant when God chose the people of Israel, he gave them many rituals and instructions to follow to worship Him. Offerings had to be brought regularly and presented according to prescribed rituals under the priests' supervision. There were special periods of corporate worship by the people of God. These included Sabbaths, new moons, and festivals. Many of these are stipulated in the book of Leviticus. The rituals, which took time to follow, offered the people of God the opportunity to prepare their hearts for worship. They were also meant to teach the people valuable lessons, such as the need to come to God with repentance, pure heart, forgiveness, and sharing fellowship with one another. Unless our hearts are pure, worship is meaningless. If we prepare our hearts and live before God with praise, thanksgiving, and worship, he will be delighted.

In the Old Testament, after a while, the people of Israel became indifferent to the meanings of these rituals, and they began to lose touch with God. God therefore was fed up with their rituals and denounced them through the prophets. Listen to Isaiah:

[10] Listen to the LORD, you leaders of Israel! Listen to the law of our God, people of Israel. You act just like the rulers and people of Sodom and Gomorrah. [11] 'I am sick of your sacrifices', says the LORD. 'Don't bring me any more burnt offerings! I don't want the fat from your rams or other animals. I don't want to see the blood from your offerings of bulls and rams and goats. [12] Why do you keep parading through my courts with your worthless sacrifices? [13] The incense you bring me is a stench in my nostrils! Your celebrations of the new moon and the Sabbath day, and your special days for fasting – even your most pious meetings – are all sinful and false. I want nothing more to do with them. [14] I hate all your festivals and sacrifices. I cannot stand the sight of them! [15] From now on, when you lift up your hands in prayer, I will refuse to look. Even though you offer many prayers, I will not listen. For your hands are covered with the blood of your innocent victims. [16] Wash yourselves and be clean! Let me no longer see your evil deeds. Give up your wicked ways. [17] Learn to do good. Seek justice. Help the oppressed. Defend the orphan. Fight for the rights of widows' (1.10-17, NLT).

Here the many sacrifices that the people were offering were worthless to God. Going through the motions of sacrifice was not enough because the people were not honouring God in their day-to-day lives: they were overlooking justice and failed to show mercy to others. This tells us that worship is genuine only when the believer is serious about the law of God. Isaiah says again, 'And so the Lord says, "These people say they are mine. They honour me with their lips, but their hearts are far away. And their worship of me amounts to nothing more than human laws learned by rote"' (Isa. 29.13, NLT).

These two texts show how important the hearts of worshippers are to God. If ours hearts are not clean, or put another way, if we are not right with God, our sacrifices are not accepted by him. Our sacrifice becomes offensive. Thus, we may spend a long time singing songs of praise and worship, but unless we are right with God, our singing amounts to nothing before God.

Worship in the New Testament

Jesus tells us the essence of true worship in his dialogue with the woman of Samaria.

> 'Sir', the woman said, 'you must be a prophet. [20] So tell me, why is it that you Jews insist that Jerusalem is the only place of worship, while we Samaritans claim it is here at Mount Gerizim, where our ancestors worshiped?' [21] Jesus replied, 'Believe me, the time is coming when it will no longer matter whether you worship the Father here or in Jerusalem. [22] You Samaritans know so little about the one you worship, while we Jews know all about him, for salvation comes through the Jews. [23] But the time is coming and is already here when true worshipers will worship the Father in spirit and in truth. The Father is looking for anyone who will worship him that way. [24] For God is Spirit, so those who worship him must worship in spirit and in truth.' (John 4.19-24, NLT).

Here Jesus tells us that there are true worshippers, and, by implication, there are also false worshippers. False worshippers are those who worship in the flesh, those who worship for worshipping's sake – but fail to worship God with their lives day by day. These people may sing, clap, kneel, or follow all the motions of worship, but it may only be formality or a show. True worshippers are those who worship God from the heart each day. God is always looking for such people.

The Samaritan woman was being challenged to be a true worshipper, because at the time she was not. She had married five times and was living with a man who was not her husband. In this story, her concern was on where, but not on whom, to worship. Both the Jews and the Samaritans placed importance on the right location of worship. The Samaritans emphasised Mount Gerizim, while the Jews emphasised the Temple in Jerusalem.

Mount Gerizim became prominent shortly after the people of Israel conquered Ai. In line with the instructions given by Moses, the people of Israel assembled at Mount Gerizim and Mount Ebal, under Joshua's direction, and there the law was read to them (Deut. 11.29-30; 27.11-13; Josh. 8.28-35). Mount Gerizim was beautiful and fertile in contrast to Mount Ebal, which was rocky and barren. Moses declared that the blessing should be proclaimed on Mount Gerizim, while the curses be proclaimed on Mount Ebal. Consequently, Mount Gerizim was associated with God's blessing while Mount Ebal was associated with God's curses. Besides this claim, Abraham once camped at Moreh, in Shechem, between Gerizim and Ebal and there received the promise that the Lord would give the land to his seed (Gen. 12.6-7). With this background, the Samaritans built a temple and worshipped there. Mount Gerizim, the mountain of blessing, was therefore very important to the Samaritans.

Jerusalem was chosen as the capital of Israel when David became king. According to Solomon, this was through divine instruction (2 Chron. 6.4-6). God had spoken centuries earlier that they should worship in the place that he would choose for them (Deut. 12.5). Making Jerusalem capital and the building of the Temple made the city very important to the Jews. It was the place of worship. The Ark of the Lord was placed in the Temple. Where the Ark was, God was. Jerusalem became the centre of worship in the Old Covenant. Thus, Jesus told the Samaritan woman, 'You Samaritans know so little about the one you worship, while we Jews know all about him, for salvation comes through the Jews' (Jn 4.22, NLT).

Jesus told the Samaritan woman, 'You need not worry about the right location of worship. You should settle you life first'. Because 'the time is coming and is already here when true worshipers will worship him wherever they are since God is spirit.' The term 'spirit' here speaks about the omnipresence of God. That is, God is spirit and is everywhere at all times. Thus, you do not need a location – a temple, a city, or country – to worship him. The true worshippers will also worship him in truth, which means they will approach him with sincere hearts. Jesus was saying that where we worship, how we worship, what we wear when we worship – are not as important as the genuineness of our worship. Worship is meaningless if the worshipper is not in right relation with God. God will be more pleased with a sincere 'Thank you, God; I love you' than with hours of singing from a dirty heart.

The Nature of Christian Worship and Praise

Paul tells us how we should pray and worship in the New Testament.

> And let the peace that comes from Christ rule in your hearts. For as members of one body you are all called to live in peace. And always be thankful. [16] Let the words of Christ, in all their richness, live in your hearts and make you wise. Use his words to teach and counsel each other. Sing psalms and hymns and spiritual songs to God with thankful hearts. [17] And whatever you do or say, let it be as a representative of the Lord Jesus, all the while giving thanks through him to God the Father (Col. 3.15-17, NLT; see also Eph. 5.1-2).

The whole of the Christian's life is intended to be devoted, in word and action, to the praise and worship of God. Although in the Old Covenant there were special periods of corporate praise and worship by the people of God, some individuals continued to praise the Lord wherever they were. The psalmist says, 'Seven times a day I praise you for your righteous laws' (Ps. 119.164, NIV). Again, he says, 'I will praise the LORD as long as I live. I will sing praises to my God even with my dying breath' (Ps. 146.2, NLT). In the New Covenant, Christians should be thankful to God always for what he has done for us.

We should be thankful to God for the salvation he has given us in Christ. This must be a major cause of our offering of praise to God. The book of Hebrews says, 'Let us, then, always offer praise to God as our sacrifice through Jesus, which is the offering presented by lips that confess him as Lord' (Heb. 13.15, GNB). Other versions, such as the New International Version and the New Living Translation use the phrase 'sacrifice of praise'. For example, the NIV reads, 'Through Jesus, therefore, let us continually offer to God a sacrifice of praise – the fruit of lips that confess his name' (13.15). The 'sacrifice of praise' includes thanking God for Christ's sacrifice on the cross and telling others about it. This act of considering his kindness and sharing it with others is pleasing to God, even when it goes unnoticed by others.

Other ways of acknowledging God's goodness and kindness in worship is appreciating what he does daily for us. God forgives our sins, heals our diseases, redeems us from death, crowns us with love and compassion, satisfies our desires, and gives us righteousness and justice (Ps. 103.1-22).

We should do this as we allow the Word of God to captivate our hearts and minds. We should sing psalms, hymns, and spiritual songs to God with thankful hearts. Our worship is to be genuine. Regarding worship music, as Paul indicated in Col. 3.15-17, we can sing biblical psalms, hymns, and choruses from our church traditions, and spiritual songs given by Holy Spirit. The psalmist said, 'Sing to the Lord a new song for he has done marvellous things' (Ps. 98.1a NIV). The combination of these three types of singing will enhance the quality of our worship. Of course worship ultimately depends upon the hearts and attitudes of worshippers toward God. Otherwise as David Servant says, 'Much of what is called worship in churches today is nothing more than dead rituals acted out by dead worshipers'.[159]

Praise and Worship Cause God to Perform Wonders

If we praise and worship God in the right way, we shall cause him to shine. If God shines, his power and strength are displayed. Moses declared, 'Who *is* like You, O LORD, among the gods? Who *is* like You, glorious in holiness, Fearful in praises, doing wonders?' (Exod. 15.11, NKJV). When God's people praise the awesomeness of God, it is his natural response to do wonders in our midst. In the song that Moses and Israel sang, God had just caused their enemies to sink. Moses realised that once God's people praise him, He does his wonders. The Lord acts against the enemies of his people, Satan and his kingdom, when His people praise Him.

Praise and Worship as Strength of God's People

The strength of God's people is praise and worship. This type of ministering to God silences the enemy. Psalm 8.2 is one of the texts which clearly brings this point out.

---

[159] Servant, *The Disciple Making Minister*, p. 282.

> Out of the mouth of babes and nursing infants You have or-
> dained strength, Because of Your enemies, That You may silence
> the enemy and the avenger. (NKJV).

> You have taught children and babies to sing praises to you be-
> cause of your enemies. And so you silence your enemies and de-
> stroy those who try to get even (New Century Version).

The term 'strength' in the King James Version has been interpreted
as 'praises' in the New Century Version. Jesus quoted this scripture
to silence the enemies who did not want the people to glorify God
when he went to Jerusalem triumphantly.

> But when the chief priests and scribes saw the wonderful things
> that He did, and the children crying out in the temple and saying,
> 'Hosanna to the Son of David!' they were indignant and said to
> Him, 'Do You hear what these are saying?' And Jesus said to
> them, 'Yes. Have you never read, "Out of the mouth of babes
> and nursing infants You have perfected praise?"' (Mt. 21.15-16,
> NKJV).

Here we realise that Jesus has interpreted the Scripture; he has re-
placed the term strength with praise. The implication is that the
strength of God's people is praise.

The King James Version is very interesting in Ps. 8.2. It has two
ways of using the term enemy. The first is 'enemies', which speaks
of Satan and his powers of evil, or his satanic kingdom. In other
words, this may be speaking about the principalities, the powers,
and the spiritual wickedness in the heavenly realms. The second is
enemy, which specifically speaks of Satan, as the head of the powers
of evil. The text 'out of the mouth' refers to the mouth as the primary source of releasing strength. What comes out of the mouth is
a weapon; it can bless or curse, give life or destroy life. The power
of the believer is in the mouth. It is not out of the month of adults,
but 'babes and nursing infants'. Babes and nursing infants represent
those who do not have natural strength of their own; they must rely
on their mothers; they are weak and feeble. Here they represent the
people of God; they do not have natural strength to combat the
devil; they must rely on God. Jesus reveals that 'babes' means his
disciples. 'At that time Jesus answered and said, "I thank You, Father, Lord of heaven and earth, that You have hidden these things

from *the* wise and prudent and have revealed them to babes'" (Mt. 11.25, NKJV).

Why has God ordained or taught his people praise and worship? The reason is clear: it is to silence his enemies and their kingdom. The enemy likes to accuse the people of God; he likes to frighten us. The book of Revelation tells us that this is the main work of the devil; he accuses believers day and night before our God (Rev. 12.10). Praise silences the enemy.

Praises of God's People are Powerful Weapons

The devil always uses schemes to promote his false ideologies. The power to destroy these includes praise. The psalmist declares:

> Let the praises of God be in their mouths, and a sharp sword in their hands – to execute vengeance on the nations and punishment on the peoples, to bind their kings with shackles and their leaders with iron chains, to execute the judgment written against them. This is the glory of his faithful ones. Praise the LORD (Ps. 149.6-9, NLT).

The people of God are commanded to be filled with the praise of God as well as the sword of the Word. This means praises and the Word of God must go together as weapons against the devil and his kingdom. Here, he was referring to Satan and his allied spirits who have been misleading the nations. Praises and the ministry of the Word of the people of God become instruments of judgment against the satanic kingdom.

Another example of the power of praise is in the Acts of Apostles, where through the praising and worshipping of Paul and Silas, prison gates got opened.

> Around midnight, Paul and Silas were praying and singing hymns to God, and the other prisoners were listening. [26]Suddenly, there was a great earthquake, and the prison was shaken to its foundations. All the doors flew open, and the chains of every prisoner fell off! [27] The jailer woke up to see the prison doors wide open. He assumed the prisoners had escaped, so he drew his sword to kill himself. [28] But Paul shouted to him, 'Don't do it! We are all here!' (Acts 16.25-28, NLT).

The enemy had succeeded in putting Paul and Silas in prison, after preaching the gospel in several days at Philippi. Meanwhile only Lydia and her household were converted (Acts 16.11-15). The result of these several days of preaching and having few converts was imprisonment of Paul and Silas. The situation appears frustrating and discouraging, but for Paul who knew the purpose of his calling and the ways of God, he and Silas were rather praising God in the prison. While praising and praying, God performed a miracle. An earthquake shook the prison and its gates opened. What power there is in praises! The jailer and his household also got converted. Oh, how I wish Christians spent much time in praises and worship and the ministration of the Word.

Summary

We have learned much about the weapons of our warfare. On the one hand, the armour of God is Jesus Christ himself. Once you put on Jesus, you have put on the full armour of God. On the other hand, if we say Jesus is all that we need, people may misunderstand what we mean. Paul's illustration about the weapons, therefore, enlighten us as to what Jesus has done for humanity. Some people divide the weapons into offensive and defensive weapons. The reason why some of the weapons – like the helmet of salvation – are termed defensive is that Roman soldiers put on the physical counterparts to defend themselves against their enemies. The offensive ones were those used to attack.

Paul compares the girdle, which in our case was considered the belt, with truth. The belt of truth was seen as our daily Christian walk with God. It demonstrates itself in sincerity, integrity, openness, frankness, and honesty. The belt of truth provides confidence for the Christian.

The breastplate of righteousness was shown as faith, the kind of faith which accepts what God has done for humankind in Christ. Jesus died to confer God's righteousness on us. The basis for granting this righteousness is God's unfailing love. Therefore, Paul also calls it the breastplate of faith and love. This weapon covers your heart from the assaults of the devil.

The shoes of the gospel of peace were found to be the preparation that was needed to know and understand the Gospel. Without such understanding, believers can be deceived. Preparation also includes the ability to communicate the Gospel. Christians must know the Gospel, experience it and present it in a simple way that should bring peace to people.

The shield of faith was presented as the faith which could be used to protect yourself and those whom the Lord has committed to your care. If the devil bombards the mind with foolish ideas, thoughts, and desires – yet fails to win you, he might attack your closest neighbour or anyone who is under your authority. Those are the times to apply the shield of faith, which is faith in Jesus, the Captain, who has defeated the devil for you.

Putting on the helmet of salvation is Paul's instruction to keep salvation as the anchor of our Christian life. Faith was shown as the ground on which believers' hope of salvation was built. The Christian hope is in God's promise (counsel), and his oath. Therefore, the Christian hope of salvation is very secure because it is impossible for God to lie; falsehood is contrary to his nature as well as to his will. The anchor which protects the Christian's hope of salvation is fastened to the Rock of Ages, which is Christ.

The sword of the Spirit, which is the Word of God is like a double-edged sword, an offensive and defensive weapon against the devil. The written Word is alive and penetrates to the deepest part of human beings. The sword of the Spirit as a defensive weapon was used in the confrontation between Satan and Jesus. Jesus repeatedly appealed to the Word of God as He resisted the devil.

Preaching and teaching were described as the ministry of the Word – the sword of the Spirit – and is a key weapon to destabilise the activities of the devil. Jesus' words to Peter at Matthew 16 are an example of the offensive nature of the church. The passage says that in the course of preaching the Gospel (i.e. Jesus is the Son of God), the devil's kingdom will try to defend itself but it will be overpowered. The preaching of the gospel is therefore one of the greatest commandments given in the Bible. In Ephesus, Paul exposed Satan and set people free in Christ by preaching the Word daily. The power of the Word healed people, cast out demons, performed extraordinary miracles, and set people free. Therefore, the Word must be preached in season and out of season.

A second facet of the sword of the Spirit is the power of testimony. In preaching we tell people about the good news of salvation, but in testimony we tell people about what we have experienced, felt or seen as a result of receiving the salvation. Testimony requires a personal experience with Jesus and the Holy Spirit. Declaring that is a power that can set people free from Satanic bondage. In Revelation believers defeated the accuser of the brethren through the blood of the lamb and the testimony of the believers.

All types of prayers are another type of weapon that must be used in the fight of faith. These include supplication (which is made for the prevention of evil), prayers (for the obtaining of good), intercessions (prayers for others), and thanksgivings (for mercies already received). I drew examples from my own devotions as a guide.

Certain Bible passages can give the impression that demons can invade – or possess – Christians, but in further reflection we saw that the verses do not really speak of possession. Therefore, the role of deliverance should be seen as part of the means of dealing with a variety of manifestations of evil in human life. But caution must be exercised. In Jesus' and Paul's ministries, they did not always resort to exorcism when confronted with evil situations. Exorcism, however, may be performed after a person has passed through a counselling session and people clearly realize that the problem is demonic.

Although Paul does not say explicitly in Ephesians 6 that one of the weapons for the warfare was praise or worship, verse 18 implies this: 'And pray in the Spirit on all occasions with all kinds of prayers and requests'. This type of life and prayer is an act of constant worship and will bring instability to the devil and his kingdom. We defined worship as placing absolute value on God and honouring Him that way, while in praising God, you renew your knowledge of God, what He has done, and what He will continue to do.

God created us for His pleasure; this was clear in the call of Israel where the Lord called them to worship him, and all the sacrificial offerings were to be acts of worship. Although God takes pleasure in our worship, he does not want us to worship him in sin. Because God is holy, His people must worship him in holiness. Yet, in the Old Testament, after a while, the people of Israel became indifferent to the meanings of these rituals of worship, and they began to lose touch with God. We may spend a long time in praises and worship, but unless our hearts are right with God, our long sessions of so-called worship amount to nothing before God.

Jesus made this clear in the Gospel of John when he declared that true worshippers must worship in truth and Spirit, which means that the place of worship, church in which we worship, the musical instruments of worship, the manner of our singing and dancing, and our clothing – are not as important as the right relationship with God in worship. Paul's writings teach that worshiping in music might include singing biblical psalms, hymns, and choruses from our church traditions, and Spirit-given songs – and all of these must be encouraged. In worship God reveals himself, and Psalm 8 teaches worship is the strength of God's people. Therefore, the people of God are commanded to be filled with the praise of God as well as the sword of the Word. This means praises and the Word of God must go together as weapons against the devil and his kingdom.

26

CONCLUSION

This study has examined the subject of spiritual warfare and responded to the challenges it raises. In Part One, I reviewed the contemporary practice of spiritual warfare and some of the blessings it has brought to Christianity. It has caused many Christians to strategise, plan, and pray better before evangelism, and many Christians have a renewed mission focus, especially on the places which encompasses a high percentage of the least-evangelised peoples in the world.

Furthermore, contemporary spiritual warfare has led many people to establish intercessory bodies, such as intercessors for Africa, AD 2000 Prayer track, and Praying Through The Window. In addition, it has exposed evil as sin that is engineered by Satan and his demons. Vices which Christians sometimes down play, such as smoking, pornography, sexual self-gratification, and gambling, are presented as the works of Satan.

The warfare concept has challenged orthodox Christians to reinvigorate their faith and practices. Consequently the contemporary approach has apparently brought revival to Christianity.

Notwithstanding the seeming strength of the contemporary spiritual warfare approach, I discussed some genuine concerns. It gives too much attention to Satan and demonic issues. Practitioners often fail to consider the sovereignty of God and the place of misfortunes in life. They interpret every mishap as demonic.

In the Bible, however, God is sometimes presented as the source of some misfortunes, and at other times, misfortunes can be attributed to neutral or natural causes. Consequently, the warfare approach has failed to understand the biblical picture of Satan. The roots of Satan's evil are his attempts to oppose God.

Another weakness is that contemporary warfare tactics relieve people from taking responsibility for their misbehaviour because Satan is considered the source of their sin. Likewise, he is blamed for all suffering. In the end, I concluded that modern spiritual warfare strategies lack a firm biblical foundation.

In Part Two, I examined what the Bible actually teaches about Spiritual warfare. We discovered that the real 'warfare' is between God and Satan. Christians are included because the human mind has become the battlefield. The Bible uses varied words to describe the contest. Ephesians calls it 'a struggle', 1 Corinthians labels it as 'warfare', and 1 Timothy identifies it as 'the fight of faith'. The scheme of the devil in the fight is to use his evil powers to plant strongholds – in the form of false doctrines, beliefs, and ideologies – in people. These are so strong that we need to preach the Word to knock them down and put on the whole armour of God to stand strong.

We established the fact that Jesus Christ has already defeated Satan in the battle. He did that through His ministry on earth, his death on the cross, and his triumphant resurrection. In the wilderness encounter with Satan, Jesus defeated Satan on his own behalf as the last Adam. Jesus' expulsion of demons during His earthly ministry was also a demonstration of his victory over Satan: the kingdom of God was breaking through satanic kingdom, and satanic powers could not withstand it.

Through the death of Jesus, Satan's hold on humanity through the power of sin has been broken. Satan held people captive because of sin. The death of Jesus which atoned for sin broke Satan's grip. The resurrection of Christ allows Jesus to apply the accomplishment of the cross and all his victories to believers.

After God has forgiven humanity our sin and delivered us from the domination of Satan, he reconciled both Jews and Gentiles in Christ to become His Church, which is His dwelling place. Through the Church God demonstrates his wisdom to the seen and unseen world. Yet, the disciples of Jesus (and all Christians) live in two worlds – the heavenly realm of Christ and the realm of the here and now. Why? The kingdom of God was inaugurated by Jesus, but His kingdom has not yet been consummated and the present world has not yet passed away. The consequence is that the two ages (the present world and the kingdom of God) are running concurrently. Christians live within these two ages, and this situation will continue until the second coming of our Lord Jesus Christ.

Many Christians have difficulty applying Jesus' victories into their daily lives. Christians have the responsibility to do this, but they can only receive the victories by faith.

In Part Three, we investigated the strongholds of the devil, which were false arguments, false philosophies, and false doctrines that result in arrogance and rebellion against God. We discussed some examples of modern-day strongholds.

The first stronghold we discussed was false doctrines – or heresy – in the Christian church. Heresy is any teaching that strays from biblical orthodoxy. To recognise whether a teaching is true or not requires that it be compared with biblical revelation. Though God's biblical revelation has been progressive, his truth never contradicts itself. False teachings can also be recognised because they are human-made rules, neglect Christ's universal church, and followers claim to be an elite or a selected group.

The second stronghold we discussed was the flesh. For Satan to succeed in opposing God, he tries to influence Christians to live in ways which are contrary to the Word of God. The flesh – or self-controlled humanity – opposes God. Christians are warned against 'the works of the flesh', because they are expressions of people living independently of God.

The postmodern philosophy was the third stronghold. Postmodernity teaches that truth is relative, dependent on circumstances. The effect of this is that everyone's viewpoint must be accommodated. The focus is on each individual's way of life. Each person must be allowed to do and practice what he or she feels is right. The media and modern technology have been the major vehicles for the promotion of postmodern ideas.

Postmodernism and the denial of absolute truth has erased the traditional, sacred view of sex and has reduced it to an ordinary act between two people. In addition, the traditional family has broken down. The home (with husband, wife, and children), previously seen as the place of refuge from a hostile public world, has been badly damaged. Parents must compete with a powerful media for the control of their children.

The New Age Movement was the fourth stronghold we discussed. It professes a broad-minded openness to all religions and
practices but is quite close-minded to the God of the Bible.

Occultism was the fifth stronghold. The occult was classified into four kinds: divination, spiritism, sorcery and magic — and also
witchcraft and astral projection.

Divination is the attempt to foresee or foretell future events, or
discover hidden knowledge by the manipulation of objects, the interpretation of omens, or with the help of supernatural power. Spiritism is the attempt to communicate with spirits. Sorcery is the use
of drugs, charms, amulets, incantations, and appeals to supernatural
powers. Witchcraft is the attempt to project one's soul with the
view to cause either good or evil. The term 'witchdemonology' describes the mingling of occult beliefs and practices with Western
Christian concepts of demonology and exorcism.

The sixth stronghold was murder. Serial killing was presented as
a dangerous example. Other dangerous strongholds here are those
strongholds that kill as a result of frustration and those that kill as a
form of revenge or even contract others to kill on their behalf as a
cover up.

The final stronghold discussed was Satanism. It was shown that
this comes up in different guises as churches or even entertaining
groups. They make mockery of God and take people's mind from
serving the true God.

In Part Four, we discussed the weapons of our warfare. Stated
simply, putting on Christ is all a Christian needs to do. But the illustration of the weapons explains what that means.

The first weapon is the belt of truth — our daily Christian walk
with God. It reveals itself in sincerity, integrity, openness, frankness,
and honesty. The belt of truth provides confidence for the Christian.

The breastplate of righteousness is faith, the kind of faith which
accepts what God has done for humankind in Christ. Jesus died to
confer God's righteousness on us. The basis for granting this righteousness is God's unfailing love. Therefore, Paul also calls it the
breastplate of faith and love. The breastplate protects the heart
from the assaults of the devil.

The shoes of the gospel of peace are the preparation that we
need to know and understand the Gospel. Without understanding

the gospel, the believer can easily be deceived. Preparation also includes the ability to communicate the gospel. Christians must know the gospel, experience it, and present it in a simple way that should bring peace to people.

The shield of faith is the faith which could be used to protect yourself and those whom the Lord has committed to your care. When the devil's attacks fail to hurt you, he might attack your closest neighbour or anyone who is under your authority. The Christian needs to apply the shield of faith in those situations.

The helmet of salvation is Paul's instruction to believers to cling to their salvation as the anchor of their Christian life. Faith is the ground on which their hope is built. The Christian hope is in God's promise (counsel), and his oath. Therefore, the Christian hope of salvation is very secure because it is impossible for God to lie. The anchor which protects the Christian hope of salvation is hammered into the Rock of Ages, which is Christ.

The sword of the Spirit, which is the Word of God is like a double-edged sword that can be used offensively and defensively against the devil. The written Word is alive and penetrates to the deepest part of human beings, and Jesus consistently referred to the Word of God when He engaged the devil.

Preaching and teaching are a key weapon to destabilise the activities of the devil. Jesus' revelation to Peter at Matthew 16 is an example of the offensive nature of the church. As we preach the Gospel – the message that Jesus is the Son of God – the devil will try to defend himself but he will not succeed. The preaching of the Gospel is therefore one of the greatest commands in the Bible. In Ephesus Paul exposed the powers of Satan and set people free by preaching the Word consistently. The power of the Word healed people, cast out demons, performed extraordinary miracles, and set people free. Therefore, the Word must be preached in season and out of season.

A second facet of the sword of the Spirit is the power of testimony. In preaching we tell people about the good news of salvation, but in testimony we tell people about what we have experienced, felt or seen as a result of receiving the salvation. Testimony requires a personal experience with Jesus and the Holy Spirit. Declaring that is a power that can set people free from Satanic bondage. In Revelation believers defeated the accuser of the brethren through the blood of the lamb and the testimony of the believers.

All types of prayers are another weapon that must be used in the fight of faith. These include supplication (which is made for the prevention of evil), prayers (for the obtaining of good), intercessions (prayers for others), and thanksgivings (for mercies already received). I drew examples from my own devotions as a guide.

Certain Bible passages can give the impression that demons can invade – or possess – Christians, but in further reflection we saw that the verses do not really speak of possession. Therefore, the role of deliverance should be seen as part of the means of dealing with a variety of manifestations of evil in human life. But caution must be exercised. In Jesus' and Paul's ministries, they did not always resort to exorcism when confronted with evil situations. Exorcism, however, may be performed after a person has passed through a counselling session and people clearly realize that the problem is demonic.

Although Paul does not say explicitly in Ephesians 6 that one of the weapons for the warfare was praise or worship, verse 18 implies this: 'And pray in the Spirit on all occasions with all kinds of prayers and requests'. This type of life and prayer is an act of constant worship and will bring instability to the devil and his kingdom. We defined worship as placing absolute value on God and honouring Him that way, while in praising God, you renew your knowledge of God, what He has done, and what He will continue to do.

God created us for His pleasure; this was clear in the call of Israel where the Lord called them to worship him, and all the sacrificial offerings were to be acts of worship. Although God takes pleasure in our worship, he does not want us to worship him in sin. Because God is holy, His people must worship Him in holiness. Yet, in the Old Testament, after a while, the people of Israel became indifferent to the meanings of these rituals of worship, and they began to lose touch with God. We may spend a long time in praises and worship, but unless our hearts are right with God, our long sessions of so-called worship amount to nothing before God.

Jesus made this clear in the Gospel of John when he declared that true worshippers must worship in truth and Spirit, which means that the place of worship, the church in which we worship, the musical instruments of worship, the manner of our singing and

dancing, and our clothing – are not as important as the right relationship with God in worship. Paul's writings teach that worshiping
in music might include singing biblical psalms, hymns, and choruses
from our church traditions, and Spirit-given songs – and all of these
must be encouraged. In worship God reveals himself, and Psalm 8
teaches worship is the strength of God's people. Therefore, the
people of God are commanded to be filled with the praise of God
as well as the sword of the Word. This means praises and the Word
of God must go together as weapons against the devil and his kingdom.

What do you need again? The battle has been defined, the
strongholds have been explained, and the weapons have been exposed to you. You need to apply the lesson and enjoy your Christian life. May the Lord God Almighty be your helper.

BIBLIOGRAPHY

Achebe, C., *The World of Ogbanje* (Enugu: Fourth Dimension, 1986).

Aker, Benny C., 'The Gospel in Action', in Benny C. Aker and Gary S. McGee (eds.), *Signs and Wonders in Ministry Today* (Springfield: Gospel Publishing House, 1996), pp. 35-45.

Allison, C. FitzSimons, *The Cruelty of Heresy* (Great Britain: SPCK, 1994).

Anderson, Allan, 'Signs and Blunders: Pentecostal Mission Issues at Home and Abroad in the 20th Century', *Asian Journal of Missions* 2.2 (2000), pp. 193-210.

Anderson, Neil, *The Bondage Breaker: Overcoming Negative Thoughts, Irrational Feelings and Habitual Sins* (London: Monarch Books, 2nd edn, 2000).

Anderson, Robert Mapes, *Vision of the Disinherited: The Making of American Pentecostalism* (Oxford: Oxford University Press, 1979).

Arnold, Clinton E., *Powers of Darkness: Principalities and Powers in Paul's Letters* (Downers Grover: InterVarsity Press, 1992).

—*Ephesians: Power and Magic. The Concept of Power in Ephesians in Light of Its Historical Setting* (Cambridge: Cambridge University Press, 1989).

—*Spirit Warfare: What Does the Bible Teach?* (London: Marshall Pickering, 1999).

Aune, David E., 'Magic, Magician', in Geoffrey Bromiley (ed.), *The International Standard Bible Encyclopedia* (Grand Rapids: Eerdmans, 1986), pp. 213-19.

Bailey, Alice, *The Externalisation of the Hierarchy* (New York: Lucis Publishing Company, 1957).

—'Esoteric Healings', in *A Treatise on the Seven Rays*, Vol. IV (New York: Lucis Publishing Company, 1953), p. 393.

Barrett, C. K., *A Critical and Exegetical Commentary on the Acts of the Apostles* (ICC; Edinburgh: T & T Clark, 1998).

Basham, Don, *Can a Christian Have a Demon?* (Monroeville: Whitaker House, 1971).

Bastian, Misty, 'Married in the Water: Spirit Kin and Other Afflictions of Modernity in Southeastern Nigerian', *Journal of Religion in Africa* 27.2 (1997), pp. 123-24.

Bittlinger, Arnold, *Gifts and Graces: A Commentary on 1 Corinthians 12-14* (Grand Rapids: Eerdmans, 1967).

Bowman, Robert M., Jr., *Understanding Jehovah's Witnesses: Why They Read the Bible the Way They Do* (Grand Rapids: Baker Book, 1991).

Bloch-Hoell, Nils, *The Pentecostal Movement: Its Origin, Development, and Distinctive Character* (London: Allen & Unwin, 1964).

Brewer, David, 'Jesus and the Psychiatrists', in Anthony N. S. Lane (ed.), *The Unseen World: Christian Reflections on Angels, Demons and the Heavenly Realms* (Carlisle: Paternoster Press, 1996), pp. 133-48.

Brown, Rebecca, *He Came to Set the Captives Free* (Springdale: Whitaker House, 1992).

—*Prepare for War* (Springdale: Whitaker House, 1987).

—*Becoming a Vessel of Honour* (Springdale: Whitaker House, 1990).

—*Unbroken Curses: Hidden Source of Trouble in the Christian's Life* (Springdale: Whitaker House, 1995).

Bruner, Frederick Dale, *A Theology of the Holy Spirit: The Pentecostal Experience and the New Testament Witness* (London: Hodder & Stoughton, 2nd edn, 1972).

Bubeck, Mark I., *Overcoming the Adversary* (Chicago: Moody Press, 1984).

—*The Adversary* (Chicago: Moody Press, 1975).

Bultmann, Rudolf, *The Gospel of John: A Commentary* (trans. G. R. Beasley-Murray, gen. ed.; Philadelphia: Westminster Press, 1971).

Carter, Steven S., 'Demon Possession and the Christian', *Asian Journal of Pentecostal Studies* 3.1 (2000), pp. 19-31.

Clark, David K. and Norman L. Geisler, *Apologetics in the New Age: A Christian Critique of Pantheism* (Grand Rapids: Baker, 1990).

Collins, Gary R., 'Psychological Observation on Demonism', in John Warwick Montgomery (ed.), *Demon Possession* (Minneapolis: Bethany House Publishers, 1976), pp. 237-51.

Conn, Charles W., *Like a Mighty Army: A History of the Church of God* (Cleveland: Pathway Press, 1977).

Cox, Harvey, *Fire From Heaven: The Rise of Pentecostal Spirituality and the Reshaping of Religion in the Twenty-First Century* (London: Cassell, 1996).

Davies, W.D. and Dale C. Allison, Jr., *A Critical and Exegetical Commentary on the Gospel According to St. Matthew* (London: Continuum Publishing Group, 2004).

Dawson, John, *Taking Our Cities for God: How to Break Spiritual Strongholds* (Lake Mary: Creation House, 1989).

Dickason, C. Fred, *Demon Possession and the Christian* (Chicago: Moody Press, 1987).

Douglas, J.D. (ed.), 'Marcion', in *New International Dictionary of the Christian Church* (Grand Rapids: Zondervan, 2nd edn, 1978), pp. 629-30.

Edward, John, *One Last Time: A Psychic Medium Speaks to those We Have Loved and Lost* (London: Piatkus, 1999).

Eni, Emmanuel, *Delivered from the Powers of Darkness* (Ibadan: Scripture Union, 1988).

Eto, Victoria, *Exposition on Water Spirit* (Warri: Christian Shalom Mission, 1988).

Evans, William, *How to Prepare Sermons* (Chicago: Moody Press, 1964).

Fee, Gordon, *God's Empowering Presence: The Holy Spirit in the Letters of Paul* (Peabody: Paternoster, 1994).

Ferdinando, Keith, 'Sickness and Syncretism in the African Context', in Anthony Billington *et al.* (eds.), *Mission and Meaning: Essays Presented to Peter Cotterell* (Carlisle: Paternoster, 1995), pp. 264-87.

—*The Triumph of Christ in African Perspective: A Study of Demonology and Redemption in the African Concept* (Carlisle: Paternoster, 1999).

—*Unmasking the New Age* (Downers Grove: InterVarsity Press, 1986).

Ferguson, Marilyn, *The Aquarian Conspiracy* (Los Angeles: J.B. Tarcher, 1980).

Gorringe, Timothy J., *Discerning of Spirits: A Theology of Revelation* (London: SCM, 1990).

Grudem, Wayne, *Systematic Theology* (Grand Rapids: Zondervan, 1994).

—*The Gift of Prophecy in 1 Corinthians* (Washington: University Press of America, 1982).

—*The Gift of Prophecy in the New Testament Today* (Eastbourne: Kingsway Publications, 1998).

Guelich, Robert A., 'Spiritual Warfare: Jesus, Paul and Peretti', *PNEUMA* 13.1 (1991), pp. 33-64.

Gundry, Robert H., *Matthew: A Commentary on His Handbook for a Mixed Church Under Persecution* (Grand Rapids: Eerdmans, 2nd edn, 1994).

Henningsen, Gustav & Bengt Ankarloo (eds.) *Early Modern European Witchcraft: Centres and Peripheries* (Oxford: Clarendon Press, 1990).

Henry, Matthew, *Matthew Henry's Commentary on the Bible* (6 Vols.; Maclean, VA: MacDonald Publishing Company, 1985).

Hertzberg, Hans Wilhelm, *1 & 11 Samuel* (Old Testament Library, trans. J. S. Bowden; London: SCM Press, 2nd edn, 1972).

Hollenweger, Walter J., *Pentecostalism: Origins and Developments Worldwide* (Peabody: Hendrickson, 1997).

—*The Pentecostals* (London: SCM Press, 1972).

Holzer, Hans, *Encyclopedia of Witchcraft and Demonology: An Illustrated Encyclopedia of Witches, Demons, Sorcerers, and Their Present-Day Counterparts* (London: Cathay Books, 1974), pp 1970-71.

Hunt, Stephen, 'Managing the Demonic: Some Aspects of the Neo-Pentecostal Deliverance Ministry', *Journal of Contemporary Religion* 13.2 (1998), pp. 215-34.

Hurtado, Larry W., *The Gospel of Mark* (New International Biblical Commentary; Carlisle: Paternoster, 1995).

Irvine, Doreen, *From Witchcraft to Christ: My True Life Story* (London: Concordia Press, 1973).

Jacobs, Cindy, *Possessing the Gates of the Enemy: A Training Manual for Militant Intercession* (Grand Rapids: Chosen, 1994).

Kalu, Ogbu U., 'The Third Response: Pentecostalism and the Reconstruction of Christian Experience in Africa, 1970-1995', *Journal of African Christian Thought* 1.2 (December 1998), pp. 3-13.

Kay, William K., *Inside Story: A History of British Assemblies of God* (Mattersey: Mattersey Hall Publishing, 1999).

Koch, Kurt E., *Occult Bondage and Deliverance* (Grand Rapids: Kregel Publications, 1970).

—*Demonology, Past and Present* (Grand Rapids: Kregel Publications, 1981).

Kraft, Charles. H., *Defeating Dark Angels* (Kent: Sovereign World, 1993).

—*Christianity with Power* (Ann Arbor, MI: Servant, 1989).

Lane, William, *The Gospel According to Mark* (The New International Commentary on the New Testament; Grand Rapids: Eerdmans, 1974).

Langley, Myrtle S., 'Spirit-Possession and Exorcism and Social Context: An Anthropological Perspective with Theological Implications', *Churchman* 94.3 (1980), pp. 226-45.

Larson, Bob, *Larson's Book of Spiritual Warfare* (Nashville: Thomas Nelson Publishers, 1999).

Lea, Tommy, 'Spiritual Warfare and the Missionary Task', in John Mark Terry, Ebbie Smith, Justice Anderson (eds.), *Missiology* (Nashville: Broadman & Holman, 1998), pp. 628-29.

Lincoln, Andrew T., *Ephesians* (Word Biblical Commentary; Nashville: Thomas Nelson, 1990).

MacNutt, Francis, *Deliverance from Evil Spirits: A Practical Manual* (London: Hodder & Stoughton, 1995).

Martin, Ralph P., *The Spirit and the Congregation: Studies in 1 Corinthians 12-15* (Grand Rapids, 1984).

Martin, Walter, *The Kingdom of the Cults* (ed. Hank Hanegraaff; Minneapolis: Bethany House Publishers, 2003).

Mauchline, John, *1 and 2 Samuel* (New Century Bible; London: Oliphants, 1971).

Maxwell, David, 'Delivered from the Spirit of Poverty? Pentecostalism, Prosperity and Modernity', *Journal of Religion in Africa* 28.3 (1998), pp. 350-73.

Meyer, Birgit, 'Delivered from the Powers of Darkness: Confessions of Satanic Riches in Christian Ghana', *Africa* 65.2 (1995), pp. 237-55.

Middleton, J. Richard and Brian J. Walsh, *Truth is Stranger Than It Used to Be: Biblical Faith in Postmodern Age* (London: SPCK, 1997).

Morris, L., 'Blood', in Walter Elwell (ed.), *Evangelical Dictionary of Theology* (Grand Rapids: Baker Books, 2nd edn, 2001), p. 175-76.

Murphy, Ed, *The Handbook for Spiritual Warfare* (Nashille: Thomas Nelson Publishing, rev. edn, 1996).

Newport, John, *The New Age Movement and the Biblical Worldview: Conflict and Dialogue* (Grand Rapids: Eerdmans Publishing Company, 1998).

Nwankpa, Emeka, *Redeeming the Land: Interceding for the Nations* (Achimota: African Christian Press, 1994).

Onyinah, Opoku, 'Matthew Speaks to Ghanaian Healing Situations', *Journal of Pentecostal Theology* 10.1 (October 2001), pp. 120-43.

—*Are Two Persons the Same: How to Overcome your Weaknesses in Temperament* (Accra: Pentecost Press Ltd, 2004).

—'Pentecostalism and the African Diaspora: An Examination of the Missions Activities of the Church of Pentecost', *PNEUMA* 26.2 (2004), pp. 216-41.

—'Contemporary 'Witchdemonology' in Africa', *International Review of Missions* 93.370/371 (October 2004), pp. 330-45.

—'Healing and Reconciliation from an African Pentecostal Perspective', in *Healing and Reconciliation: Pastoral Counseling Across Christian Traditions Cultures* (CWME: Athens, 2005), pp. 35-41.

Oshun, Chris O., 'Spirits and Healing in a Depressed Economy: The Case of Nigeria', *Mission Studies* 25.1 (1998), pp. 32-52.

Otis, George, Jr., *The Last of the Giants: Lifting the Veil on Islam and the End Times* (Grand Rapids: Chosen, 1993).

—'An Overview of Spiritual Mapping', in C. Peter Wagner (ed.), *Breaking Strongholds in Your City: How to Use Spiritual Mapping to Make Prayers More Strategic, Effective, and Targeted* (Ventura: Regal, 1991), pp. 29-47.

Parker, Stephen E., *Led by the Spirit: Toward a Practical Theology of Pentecostal Discernment and Decision Making* (JPTSup, 7; Sheffield: Sheffield Academic Press, 1996).

Patzia, Arthur G., *Ephesians, Colossians, Philemon* (New International Biblical Commentary; Peabody, MA: Hendrickson, 1990).

Peretti, Frank, *This Present Darkness* (Westchester: Crossway Books, 1986).

Powlison, David, *Power Encounters: Reclaiming Spiritual Warfare* (Grand Rapid: Baker Books, 1995).

Prince, Derek, *Blessings or Cursing* (Milton Keynes: Word Publishing, 1990).

—*From Cursing to Blessing* (Lauderdale: Derek Prince Ministries, 1986).

—*They Shall Expel Demons: What You Need to Know about Demons: Your Invisible Enemies* (Harpenden: Derek Prince Ministries, 1998).

Rallo, Vito, *Breaking Generational Curses & Pulling Down Strongholds* (Lake Mary: Creation House Press, 2000).

Richards, John, *But Deliver Us from Evil: An Introduction to the Demonic Dimension in Pastoral Care* (London: Darton, 1974).

—*Exorcism Deliverance and Healing: Some Pastoral and Liturgical Guidelines* (Nottingham: Grove Books Limited, 3rd edn, 1990).

Ridenour, Fritz, *So What's the Difference?* (Ventura: Regal Books, 1979).

Sampson, Philip, 'The Rise of Postmodernity', in Philip Sampson, Vinay Samuel, and Chris Sugden (eds.), *Faith and Modernity* (Oxford: Regum, 1994), pp. 29-57.

Seaman, Barrett, 'Good Heaven! An Astrologer Dictating the President's Schedule?' *Time Magazine* (May 16, 1988), Available at: http://www.time.com/time/magazine/article/0,9171,967389,00.html. Accessed: November 19, 2007.

Servant, David, *The Disciple Making Minister: Biblical Principles for Fruitful and Multiplication* (Pittsburgh: Ethnos Press, 2005).

—*The Great Gospel Deception: Exposing the False Promise of Heaven Without Holiness* (Pittsburgh: Ethnos Press, 1999).

Shaw, Gwen, *Redeeming the Land: A Bible Study on Dislodging Evil Spirits, Breaking the Curse and Restoring God's Blessing Upon the Land* (Japer, Arkansas, 1987).

Slate, Joe H., *Astral Projection and Psychic Empowerment: Techniques for Mastering the Out-of-Body Experience* (St Paul, Minnesota: Llewellyn Publications, 1998).

Stibbs, A.M. 'The Pastoral Epistles', in D. Guthrie *et al.* (eds.), *The New Bible Commentary: Revised* (Leicester: Inter-Varsity Press, 1970.), pp. 1166-86.

Subritsky, Bill, *Demons Defeated* (Chichester: Sovereign World, 1986).

Suenens, Leon-Joseph, *Renewal and the Powers of Darkness* (Darton: Longman, Todd, and Servant Publications, 1983).

Towns, Elmer L., *What the Faith is All About: A Study of the Basic Doctrines of Christianity* (Wheaton: Tyndale House Publishers, 1983).

Twelftree, Graham, *Christ Triumphant: Exorcism Then and Now* (London: Hodder & Stoughton, 1985).

—'The Place of Exorcism in Contemporary Ministry', *St Mark's Review* 127 (1986), pp. 25-39.

Ugwu, Chinonyelu Moses, *Healing in the Nigerian Church: A Pastoral-Psychological Exploration* (Bern: Peter Lang, 1998).

Unger, Merrill F., *What Demons Can Do to Saints* (Chicago: Moody Press, 1977).

Wagner, C. Peter, *Warfare Prayer* (Ventura: Regal, 1991).

—*Warfare Prayer: How to Seek God's Power and Protection in the Battle to Build His Kingdom* (Ventura: Regal, 1992).

— *Confronting the Powers: How the New Testament Church Experienced the Power of Strategic Level Spiritual Warfare* (Ventura: Regal, 1996).

Wagner, C. Peter (ed.), *Engaging the Enemy: How to Fight and Defeat Territorial Spirits* (Ventura: Regal, 1993).

Wakely, Mike, 'Territorial Spirits: Some Concerns Expressed by Mike Wakely', Operation Mobilization (18 July 1993).

Warrington, Keith, 'Healing and Exorcism: The Path to Wholeness', in Keith Warrington (ed.), *Pentecostal Perspective* (Carlisle: Paternoster Press, 1998), pp. 147-76.

White, John, 'Commentary on Psychological Observation in Demonism', in John Warwick Montgomery (ed.), *Demon Possession* (Minneapolis: Bethany House Publishers, 1976), pp. 252-55.

Williamson, Linda, *Contacting the Spirit World: How to Develop Your Psychic abilities and Stay in Touch with Loved Ones* (London: Piatkus, 1996).

Wimber, John with Kevin Springer, *Power Evangelism* (London; Hodder and Stoughton, 1992).

Wimber, John and Kevin Springer, *Power Healing* (London: Hodder & Stoughton, 1988).

Index of Biblical References

Index of Authors

Made in the USA
Middletown, DE
01 October 2016